DIVERSITY

V.I.B.E.S.

Valuing, Inclusion, Belonging, Equity, and Social Justice

Table of Contents

"We may have all come on different ships, but we're in the same boat now."

- **Martin Luther King Jr.**

As I live today as a "Baby Boomer" I was intentionally discriminated in my Mother's womb as she and my fore parents faced the injustices and prejudices that came with Jim Crow and Segregation. You see, I was born a Negro boy and would be referred to as Colored, later to be classified as Black, then only to be reclassified as African- American because of my beautiful Melanated skin that many non-bipoc (Black, Indigenous, People of Color) lay out in the sun with an attempt to look like me as I continue to bring V.I.B.E.S. to all that I encounter.

Diversity, Inclusion, Belonging, and Social Justice are four key elements that are crucial to creating an equitable and inclusive society. These elements are very closely aligned and interconnected and work in tandem to create an environment where people from all walks of life feel valued, included, and a sense of belonging. In this essay, we will explore the concept of Diversity V.I.B.E.S, which stands for Valuing, Inclusion, Belonging, and Social Justice, and how this framework can be applied in various settings to promote diversity and social equity.

Valuing diversity is the first element of Diversity V.I.B.E.S. It is about recognizing and appreciating the differences in individuals, including but not limited to race, ethnicity, gender, sexual orientation, religion, socio-economic status, and ability. Valuing diversity means understanding that each person brings a unique perspective and set of experiences to the table, and that these differences are to be celebrated rather than marginalized.

By valuing diversity, individuals and organizations can foster a culture of respect and appreciation that encourages collaboration, innovation, and creativity.

Inclusion is the second element of Diversity V.I.B.E.S. It goes beyond simply recognizing diversity and extends to actively involving and engaging individuals from diverse backgrounds in decision making processes and opportunities. Inclusion means creating a space where everyone feels welcomed, supported, and respected, and where their voices are heard and valued.

This requires intentional efforts to remove barriers to participation and to create a culture that actively seeks out and promotes the contributions of all individuals, regardless of their differences.

Belonging is the third element of Diversity V.I.B.E.S. It is about creating an environment where individuals feel a sense of connection, cohesion, and membership. Belonging means that everyone feels like they are an integral part of the community or organization, and that their presence and contributions are essential to its success. When individuals feel like they belong, they are more likely to be engaged, motivated, and committed, leading to greater satisfaction and productivity. Establishing a sense of belonging requires not only valuing diversity and promoting inclusion, but also creating a culture that is supportive, empathetic, and nurturing.

Social Justice is the fourth element of Diversity V.I.B.E.S

It is about addressing the systemic inequalities and injustices that exist in society and working towards creating a fair and equitable world for all individuals, particularly those who have been historically marginalized and oppressed. Social justice requires actively challenging discrimination and prejudice, advocating for the rights of marginalized communities, and working towards policies and practices that promote equality and accessibility. It also involves acknowledging and addressing the ways in which power and privilege operate within institutions and systems, and working towards dismantling barriers and creating opportunities for all individuals to thrive.

As I continue to walk uprightly before God and Mankind, I see the sermon everyday as Diversity V.I.B.E.S provides a comprehensive framework for promoting diversity and social equity in various settings, including workplaces, educational institutions, and communities.

By valuing diversity, promoting inclusion, fostering belonging, and advocating for social justice, individuals and organizations can create environments where everyone feels valued, included, and supported, and where opportunities for success are accessible to all.

It is essential for individuals and organizations to actively engage with this framework in order to create a more equitable and inclusive society for future generations.

The world is a beautifully diverse place. It is made up of people with various backgrounds, traditions, and beliefs. This diversity should be cherished and celebrated, as it brings a rich array of ideas, perspectives, and experiences to the table. However, it is important to acknowledge that not all individuals are afforded the same opportunities, respect, and recognition. This is where Diversity, Equity, Inclusion, and Belonging (DEIB) come into play.

DEIB is a framework that aims to create a culture where every individual is acknowledged and supported, regardless of their differing background. It goes beyond simply tolerating or accepting diversity; it seeks to actively embrace and value it. DEIB recognizes that each person has a unique set of experiences and insights to offer, and by fostering an inclusive environment, these diverse voices can be heard and valued. It encompasses various individual differences, such as gender, race, religion, ethnicity, or sexual orientation, among others.

Introduction

In today's globalized world, where collaboration and innovation are key drivers of success, organizations that prioritize DEIB - Diversity V.I.B.E.S are more likely to thrive. A diverse workplace brings together individuals from different walks of life, who can offer fresh perspectives and solutions to problems. When people with differing backgrounds come together, they bring with them a wealth of knowledge and experiences that can spark creativity and innovation. This can lead to better decision-making and problem-solving, as different perspectives challenge the status quo and offer new approaches.

Moreover, DEIB fosters a sense of belonging for individuals. It is not enough to simply have diversity within an organization; individuals must also feel included and valued for their contributions. When people feel a sense of belonging, they are more likely to be engaged, motivated, and committed to their work. This, in turn, leads to increased productivity and job satisfaction. DEIB also helps to address disparities and inequities that exist in society, ensuring that all individuals have equitable opportunities and access to resources within the workplace.

To achieve DEIB, organizations must actively work towards creating an inclusive and equitable culture. This can be done through various means, such as inclusive language and leadership. Language is a powerful tool that can either perpetuate or challenge biases and stereotypes. Using inclusive language that respects and affirms diverse identities and experiences is crucial in creating an inclusive workplace.

Similarly, leadership plays a vital role in setting the tone and creating an environment where diversity and inclusion are valued and practiced. Leaders must lead by example and ensure that policies, practices, and decision-making processes are fair and unbiased.

Additionally, organizations can provide training and education on DEIB to their employees. This can help individuals recognize their own biases and learn how to respond to microaggressions and discriminatory behavior. DEIB training can also provide resources and guidance on how to create a safe and welcoming work environment for everyone.

It is important to note that DEIB is an ongoing journey, and organizations must continually evaluate and update their practices to ensure continued progress.

Diversity, Equity, Inclusion, Belonging, and Social Justice are essential elements for creating a thriving workplace culture. Organizations that prioritize DEIB benefit from the different perspectives and unique contributions of their employees. A diverse and inclusive workplace fosters innovation, creativity, and better decision-making.

It also cultivates a sense of belonging and ensures that all individuals have equal opportunities to succeed.

Through inclusive language, leadership, and training, organizations can create an environment where every individual is acknowledged, supported, and encouraged to evolve both personally and professionally. By embracing DEIB - Diversity V.I.B.E.S, we create a better future for everyone.

Prioritizing diversity, equity, inclusion, and belonging (DEIB) in the workplace has numerous benefits that positively impact the organization's culture, productivity, and bottom line. Here are some key benefits and contributions:

1.   **Increased innovation and creativity:** DEIB brings together individuals with diverse perspectives, backgrounds, and experiences, fostering a multicultural and inclusive environment. This diversity of thought stimulates creativity, leading to the generation of new ideas, perspectives, and approaches. It encourages employees to challenge norms, think differently, and explore innovative solutions to business challenge

2.Enhanced problem-solving and decision-making: When diverse voices and experiences are included in decision-making processes, organizations can access a wider range of insights and expertise. This diversity helps identify blind spots, mitigates group think, and encourages robust discussions. By considering multiple perspectives, teams can make more informed decisions and achieve better outcomes.

3. Improved adaptability and flexibility: Inclusive workplaces embrace different ways of thinking and diverse work styles. This nurtures adaptability, as employees learn to navigate alternative approaches and viewpoints. The ability to adapt and be flexible is crucial in today's rapidly changing business landscape, where organizations need to respond to diverse customer needs and market shifts more effectively.

3. Broader talent pool and recruitment advantages: Prioritizing DEIB in the workplace expands the pool of potential talent and enables organizations to attract diverse candidates who represent a variety of backgrounds and experiences. This leads to a broader range of skills, perspectives, and ideas within the workforce, enriching the organization's capacity to innovate, problem-solve, and connect with diverse customer bases.

4. Increased employee engagement and retention: Creating an inclusive environment where all employees feel respected, valued, and included results in higher levels of employee engagement and satisfaction. People feel more motivated to contribute their best, leading to increased productivity and reduced turnover. Inclusive organizations recognize and celebrate the unique qualities of each employee, fostering a sense of belonging and loyalty.

5. Better understanding of customer needs: A diverse workforce can relate to and understand the needs, preferences, and challenges of a broader range of customers

Chapter One:

V.I.B.E.S - Opening the Doors to Diversity, Equity, Inclusion, and Belonging

Overall, prioritizing diversity, equity, inclusion, and belonging in the workplace fosters an environment that unlocks the full potential of individuals and teams, resulting in enhanced innovation, creativity, decision-making, and overall business success. In the pursuit of creating a diverse, equitable, and inclusive organization, it is crucial to differentiate between equity and equality. While equality aims to ensure that everyone is treated the same, regardless of their individual circumstances, equity acknowledges that different individuals require different levels of support and resources to achieve an equal outcome.

Equality operates under the assumption that individuals are starting from the same point and have the same needs. It promotes a "one size fits all" approach, where everyone is given the same resources and opportunities. While equality is an important value to uphold in society, it does not account for the systemic barriers and unequal opportunities that exist for different individuals. It fails to address the unique circumstances and needs of marginalized groups, perpetuating existing inequalities.

Equity, on the other hand, recognizes that individuals come from different backgrounds and face different barriers. It acknowledges that certain groups may require additional support and resources to level the playing field and ensure equal opportunities. Equity seeks to address the systemic barriers and power imbalances that contribute to unequal outcomes. By providing support, assistance, and opportunities based on individual needs, equity aims to create a fair and impartial system.

The goal of equity is not to treat everyone exactly the same, but rather to ensure that everyone has an equal opportunity to succeed. It takes into account the historical disadvantages and systemic biases that certain groups face, and seeks to rectify these inequalities. By addressing the root causes of inequity and providing targeted support, equity can help create a more inclusive and just society.

In the context of organizations, equity is essential for creating a workplace where everyone has an equal chance to thrive. It involves recognizing and addressing any biases or barriers that may exist within the organization.

This may include implementing policies and practices that promote equal opportunities for advancement, creating mentorship programs, or providing training on unconscious bias.

Diversity, Equity, Inclusion, and Belonging are crucial concepts in creating a workplace that values and celebrates the unique contributions of every individual. Equity, as opposed to equality, recognizes and addresses the different needs and barriers that exist for marginalized groups.

By providing targeted support and resources, organizations can create a culture of fairness and impartiality. In doing so, they promote an environment where all employees feel valued, included, and empowered to succeed. Through the implementation of DEIS principles, organizations can unlock the full potential of their diverse workforce, leading to greater success and growth.

By embracing equity, organizations can foster a culture of inclusivity and belonging. Employees will feel supported and valued for their unique contributions, regardless of their background or circumstances. This, in turn, can lead to increased productivity, innovation, and overall success for the organization.

In the pursuit of creating a diverse, equitable, and inclusive organization, it is crucial to differentiate between equity and equality. While equality aims to treat everyone the same, equity recognizes and addresses the different needs and barriers that exist for marginalized groups.

By embracing equity, organizations can create a culture of fairness, impartiality, and inclusion, leading to numerous benefits including increased creativity, improved decision-making, enhanced employee engagement and productivity, a broader talent pool, improved reputation, and reduced legal and ethical risks.

Embracing diversity, equity, inclusion, and belonging is not just the right thing to do, it is also the smart thing to do for the success and growth of any organization.

1. **Diversity:** Diversity refers to the presence of a wide range of individuals with different characteristics, backgrounds, perspectives, and identities within an organization. This can include differences in race, ethnicity, gender, age, sexual orientation, religion, disability status, socioeconomic background, and more. Embracing diversity ensures a variety of viewpoints, experiences, and skills, which can lead to increased creativity, innovation, and problem-solving capabilities in the workplace.

2. **Equity:** Equity emphasizes fairness and justice in removing barriers and providing equal opportunities for all individuals. It recognizes that people have different starting points and need different resources and support to achieve equitable outcomes. Achieving equity involves identifying and addressing systemic and structural inequalities that may exist within an organization, which can result in a more inclusive and level playing field for everyone.

3. **Inclusion:** Inclusion focuses on creating an environment where all individuals feel respected, valued, and included, regardless of their differences. It involves fostering a culture that promotes collaboration, belongingness, and a sense of community where diverse perspectives are welcomed and appreciated. Inclusion encourages active participation, engagement, and the ability for individuals to bring their authentic selves to work, leading to higher job satisfaction, productivity, and retention rates.

4. **Belonging:** Belonging refers to an individual's sense of comfort, acceptance, and connection within a workplace culture. It goes beyond being included, as it signifies a feeling of being an integral part of the organization, where one's contributions are recognized and appreciated. When individuals feel a sense of belonging, they are more likely to fully engage, contribute their unique perspectives, and thrive in their personal and professional development.

All four concepts are essential in creating a successful workplace culture because they complement and reinforce each other. Diversity brings in varied perspectives, experiences, and talent. Equity ensures fairness, promotes equal opportunities, and removes systemic barriers. Inclusion fosters a positive and collaborative environment that encourages participation and engagement. Belonging ensures that every individual feels valued, respected, and connected.

By combining all these elements, organizations can benefit from enhanced creativity, innovation, engagement, employee satisfaction, productivity, and ultimately, a more successful overall performance. Promoting diversity in the workplace and ensuring inclusivity and equity for everyone requires a proactive and comprehensive approach from organizations.

Here are some strategies to achieve these goals:

1. **Establish a diverse and inclusive culture:** Organizations should develop a clear commitment to diversity and inclusion, starting from the top leadership. Foster a culture that values and celebrates different perspectives, backgrounds, and experiences.

2. **Educate and raise awareness:** Conduct diversity and inclusion training programs for employees at all levels, focusing on unconscious bias, cultural sensitivity, and respectful communication. This helps create awareness about diversity issues and promotes a more inclusive workplace.

3. **Implement diverse hiring practices:** Establish diverse hiring practices that attract candidates from diverse backgrounds. Review and revise job descriptions to avoid biased language and ensure they focus on essential skills rather than specific qualifications that may exclude certain groups.

4. **Build diverse teams:** Encourage diverse representation within teams and across different levels of the organization. This fosters a more inclusive work environment and encourages collaboration and innovation.

5. Provide equal opportunities for advancement: Create systems that allow all employees, regardless of back ground, to access opportunities for professional growth and advancement. Establish mentorship or sponsorship programs to support underrepresented employees and provide them with guidance and exposure.

6. Review policies and procedures: Regularly assess policies and procedures to identify and remove any potential barriers or biases that could hinder diversity and inclusivity. This includes evaluating recruitment and promotion processes, pay structures, and work-life balance policies.

7. Offer employee resource groups: Establish employee resource groups (ERGs) or affinity groups to provide a platform for employees to connect, seek support, and share experiences based on their backgrounds or identities. These groups can help foster a sense of belonging and provide insights to improve the overall workplace experience.

8. Encourage open and respectful communication: Create an environment where employees feel safe to speak up, share their experiences, and provide feedback on diversity-related issues. Encourage dialogue and active listening to ensure all voices are heard and valued.

9. Continuously measure and track progress: Regularly collect data on diversity and inclusion indicators, such as representation, retention, and employee satisfaction. Analyze this data to identify gaps and areas for improvement, and use it to set goals and measure progress over time.

10. Hold leaders accountable: Ensure that leaders and managers actively support and promote diversity and inclusion initiatives.

Hold them accountable for creating an inclusive, equitable work environment through performance evaluations, regular feedback, and recognition of their efforts.

By implementing these strategies, organizations can effectively promote diversity, foster inclusivity, and create a workplace that is equitable and supportive for all employees.

Chapter Two:

Dimensions of Diversity - Cleaning Your Lens

The "Dimensions of Diversity" explores the various dimensions of diversity in the workplace. This chapter highlights the importance of recognizing and valuing differences among employees in terms of race, ethnicity, ability, gender, and age. It emphasizes the benefits of building a diverse team and the need to address issues such as racism, ethnic discrimination, ableism, sexism, and ageism.

Racial diversity is one of the most common dimensions of diversity. It involves acknowledging and celebrating differences in race and shared physical and social traits. A racially diverse workforce brings about innovation, adaptability, and improved team collaboration. Research has shown that diverse teams are more likely to come up with creative solutions to problems and make better decisions. Employees from different racial backgrounds bring unique perspectives and experiences that can contribute to a more comprehensive understanding of customer needs and preferences. By embracing racial diversity, organizations can also tap into a larger talent pool and attract a wider range of customers.

However, racial discrimination can still exist in the workplace and is often seen through racially insensitive jokes, derogatory language, or preferential treatment for promotions. Racial discrimination not only harms individuals but also undermines teamwork and productivity.

To prevent racial discrimination, it is essential to understand racial diversity and work towards creating an inclusive and respectful workplace. This can include implementing diversity training programs, fostering open dialogue about race, and establishing policies that promote diversity and equality.

Ethnic diversity, although often used interchangeably with race, carries a distinct meaning. Ethnicity is based on cultural identity and learned behaviors. It encompasses religion, language, dress, and nationality. Embracing ethnic diversity in the workplace brings diverse viewpoints, higher productivity, and personal and professional growth opportunities.

Research has shown that a multicultural work environment can lead to increased creativity and innovation due to the exposure to different perspectives and approaches to problem-solving.

Organizations that promote ethnic diversity also enjoy a competitive advantage by being able to cater to a broader customer base. Improving cultural awareness and connecting with individuals on a personal level are crucial in promoting ethnic diversity in the workplace. Organizations can foster an inclusive culture by celebrating cultural events and holidays, providing diversity training, and creating opportunities for employees to learn about different cultures;

By embracing ethnic diversity, organizations can create a vibrant and dynamic work environment that values and respects individuals' cultural backgrounds. Ability diversity refers to differences in abilities and disabilities. Disability can manifest in physical, sensory, mental, and behavioral forms. Individuals with disabilities often face stigma and negative beliefs, which can lead to exclusion and discrimination in the workplace. Building an inclusive workplace involves proper accommodations to help disabled employees integrate into the work environment. This can include making physical modifications such as ramps or accessible restrooms, providing assistive technologies, and implementing flexible work arrangements. Inclusive hiring practices, mental support, and equal opportunities for career advancement are also essential for creating a welcoming and accessible workplace for individuals with disabilities.

Gender diversity encompasses physical sex, gender identity, assigned sex, perceived gender, and gender presentation. An inclusive workplace accommodates all genders, promoting fairness and safety for everyone. Gender diversity brings multiple perspectives, enhances group collaboration, and improves recruitment and reputation.

Research has shown that companies with more diverse gender representation in leadership positions tend to have higher financial returns.

Gender diversity initiatives can include implementing gender-neutral policies, providing parental leave for all genders, and promoting equal pay for equal work. Creating a safe and supportive work environment free from gender discrimination is crucial for retaining and attracting top talent.

Sexism, or gender discrimination, is a form of prejudice or discrimination based on sex or gender. It can manifest through the gender pay gap, denial of promotions, or unequal treatment. Combating sexism requires equal opportunities for all genders and promoting a culture of respect and equality. Inclusive leadership that actively addresses gender bias and promotes gender diversity is crucial in tackling sexism in the workplace.

Age diversity recognizes the value that individuals from different generations bring to the workplace. Different age groups provide unique perspectives, working styles, and preferences. Embracing age diversity leads to increased productivity and innovation. Older employees bring experience, while younger employees contribute fresh ideas. Research has shown that age-diverse teams are more likely to foster creativity and problem-solving. Age diversity also helps organizations better understand and connect with different age segments in their customer base.

Ageism is a negative bias based on age. It can occur at any age but is more common among young workers starting their careers or older employees approaching retirement. Ageism manifests through age-specific comments, unequal distribution of benefits, or limited opportunities for younger employees to learn from experienced colleagues.

Overcoming ageism involves treating employees of all ages with fairness and respect, valuing their contributions, and creating opportunities for collaboration and knowledge sharing across generations. Organizations can establish mentoring programs, reverse mentoring initiatives, and cross generational teamwork to foster a culture of intergenerational collaboration.

The dimensions of diversity in the workplace encompass race, ethnicity, ability, gender, and age. Embracing these dimensions brings numerous benefits to organizations, such as innovation, adaptability, and improved team collaboration. However, it is crucial to address issues such as racism, ethnic discrimination, ableism, sexism, and ageism to create an inclusive and respectful workplace.

By valuing and celebrating differences, organizations can create a vibrant and diverse work environment that attracts top talent, engages employees, and fosters creativity and innovation.

In today's diverse world, workplace diversity is not only important but also necessary for the success and innovation of an organization. A workplace culture is shaped by its employees and their unique traits, abilities, and backgrounds.

These differences, or dimensions of diversity, set individuals apart from one another and contribute to a creative and successful team. While some dimensions of diversity are visible, others are not immediately apparent. In this essay, we will explore four dimensions of diversity: racial diversity, ethnic diversity, ability diversity, and gender diversity.

Racial diversity is one of the most common dimensions of diversity. It involves acknowledging and celebrating differences in race and shared physical and social traits.

These physical traits can include skin color, hair or eye color, facial structure, and other characteristics that originate from an individual's geographic location or genetic background. A racially diverse workforce consists of employees from various racial backgrounds, allowing for increased innovation, adaptability, flexibility, and improved team collaboration. Unfortunately, racial discrimination still exists in the workplace, with acts of racism or racial discrimination encompassing restrictions or exclusions based on color, race, or descent.

Understanding racial diversity is crucial in preventing racial discrimination and creating an inclusive work environment. Ethnic diversity, although often overlapping with race, has distinct meanings. Ethnicity is based on learned behaviors and an individual's cultural identity, which can include religion, language, dress, and nationality.

Embracing ethnic diversity in the workplace offers benefits such as diverse viewpoints for economic development, higher productivity, and personal and professional growth opportunities.

To foster ethnic diversity, it is vital to commit to improving cultural awareness and creating personal connections with individuals from different ethnic backgrounds. To build an inclusive workplace, it is essential to consider individuals with disabilities and provide proper accommodations, such as inclusive hiring practices, mental support, and physical accommodations.

Prioritizing ability diversity creates a welcoming and accessible workplace that promotes acceptance and understanding. Ability diversity refers to the differences in ability and various types of disabilities. Disabilities can encompass physical, sensory, mental, and behavioral impairments. Unfortunately, disability often carries a stigma and negative beliefs, which can hinder integration into the work environment.

Gender diversity involves fair representation of people belonging to different gender groups and encompasses physical sex, gender identity, assigned sex, perceived gender, and gender presentation. In an inclusive culture, gender diversity ensures a safe environment for all employees, regardless of their gender. It allows for balanced hiring rates, equal working opportunities, and fair pay and appreciation.

Gender diversity is highly beneficial in the workplace as it provides multiple perspectives, boosts collaboration, and enhances recruitment and the company's reputation. However, sexism, which is prejudice or discrimination based on sex or gender, remains a prevalent issue. It manifests in actions, laws, and media representations that favor one gender over another. Overcoming sexism and gender discrimination requires addressing the gender pay gap, promoting equal opportunities for promotion, and treating all genders as equally competent.

Age diversity recognizes the value that individuals from different generations bring to the workplace. Each generation has its own perspectives, working styles, and preferences shaped by their unique experiences. Diverse age groups foster productivity, innovation, and problem solving by incorporating different worldviews.

Ageism, however, remains a challenge, targeting individuals on the basis of their age. Ageism can manifest as negative attitudes, assumptions, unequal distribution of benefits, or limited opportunities for younger and older employees. Creating an inclusive workplace that values age diversity involves challenging age-specific biases and providing equal opportunities for growth and development.

Workplace diversity is not only important but also necessary for the success and innovation of an organization in today's diverse world.

Four dimensions of diversity, namely racial diversity, ethnic diversity, ability diversity, and gender diversity, play pivotal roles in creating an inclusive work environment. Workplace diversity encompasses various dimensions, including racial diversity, ethnic diversity, ability diversity, gender diversity, and age diversity. A diverse and inclusive workplace recognizes and values these dimensions, leading to increased innovation, adaptability, and collaboration.

By embracing these dimensions of diversity and addressing issues such as discrimination and stereotypes, organizations can foster creativity, collaboration, and productivity, leading to long term success. It is imperative for companies to recognize the value of diversity and actively work towards creating an inclusive workplace culture. To create an inclusive environment that fosters diversity, it is crucial to address issues such as racial discrimination, ethnic bias, ableism, gender discrimination, and ageism. Embracing diversity and its dimensions promotes personal and professional growth, fosters creativity and success, and ultimately benefits individuals, organizations, and society as a whole.

The inclusion of individuals with disabilities and providing proper accommodations in the workplace can contribute to a more welcoming and accessible environment in several ways:

1. **Diverse talent pool:** By including individuals with disabilities, employers tap into a wider talent pool and benefit from the unique skills and perspectives they bring. This diversity can foster innovation, creativity, and problem-solving within the workplace.

2. **Increased employee morale:** Creating a workplace that is inclusive and accommodating fosters a positive work culture. When employees see that their organization values diversity and makes efforts to create an accessible environment, it boosts morale and creates a sense of belonging for all employees.

3. **Improved productivity:** With proper accommodations, individuals with disabilities can fully participate and contribute to their full potential. Accessible technology, reasonable adjustments, and accommodations empower employees to perform their tasks efficiently, leading to increased productivity.

Practical Illustration

Susan is new in her company, and has been tasked to help update the company's safety plan. In her old job, Susan was involved in many group projects with men who never let her speak or express her opinions. She was nervous, because she was not yet familiar with her new coworkers. During their first meeting, Susan's coworkers greeted and welcomed her to the team. They each took turns adding ideas to the safety plan. Tom, who had been with the company for years and had vast experience with the planning, offered to organize the written layout of the plan. Norris, who is also new with the company, suggested that he could use Tom's written copy of the plan and create an online version to share with everyone, since he is great at technology.

When it came time for Susan to contribute her thoughts, she suggested the idea of upgrading the fire alarm system, to one that includes lights or alerts. She explained that she is hard of hearing, and that it would be helpful to have if she is not wearing her hearing aids, or if other individuals who are deaf or hard of hearing are in the building. Everyone listened carefully to Susan's ideas, and thanked her for sharing. Susan was happy to see such great teamwork amongst a diverse group of individuals and perspectives.

In today's complex and diverse world, workplace diversity is not only important but also necessary for the success and innovation of an organization. A workplace culture is shaped by its employees and their unique traits, abilities, and backgrounds. These differences, or dimensions of diversity, set individuals apart from one another and contribute to a creative and successful team. While some dimensions of diversity are visible, others are not immediately apparent. In this book, we will explore four dimensions of diversity: racial diversity, ethnic diversity, ability diversity, and gender diversity. Racial diversity involves acknowledging and celebrating differences in race and shared physical and social traits. A racially diverse workforce consists of employees from various racial backgrounds, allowing for increased innovation, adaptability, flexibility, and improved team collaboration. Understanding racial diversity is crucial in preventing racial discrimination and creating an inclusive work environment.

Ethnic diversity, although often overlapping with race, has distinct meanings. Embracing ethnic diversity in the workplace offers benefits such as diverse viewpoints for economic development, higher productivity, and personal and professional growth opportunities. To foster ethnic diversity, it is vital to committing to improving cultural awareness and creating personal connections with individuals from different ethnic backgrounds.

Ability diversity refers to the differences in ability and various types of disabilities. To build an inclusive workplace, it is essential to consider individuals with Gender diversity involves fair representation of people belonging to different gender groups. In an inclusive culture, gender diversity ensures a safe environment for all employees, regardless of their gender. It allows for balanced hiring rates, equal working opportunities, and fair pay and appreciation. Overcoming sexism and gender discrimination requires addressing the gender pay gap, promoting equal opportunities for promotion, and treating all genders as equally competent. Age diversity recognizes the value that individuals from different generations bring to the workplace.

Each generation has its own perspectives, working styles, and preferences shaped by their unique experiences. Diverse age groups foster productivity, innovation, and problem- solving by incorporating different worldviews.

Creating an inclusive workplace that values age diversity involves challenging age- specific biases and providing equal opportunities for growth and development.

In conclusion, workplace diversity is crucial in today's diverse world. By embracing and celebrating dimensions of diversity such as race, ethnicity, ability, gender, and age, organizations can create an inclusive and successful workplace culture. It is not only important but also necessary for organizations to promote diversity and create an environment that encourages the success and innovation that comes from a diverse team.

"I always say that Sunday is the most segregated day in society as people from all walks of life go their separate ways to worship."

J. Lamont Harris 2020

Chapter Three:

Dimensions of Diversity- Calibrating Your Lens

Diversity is a fundamental aspect of the human experience. In every aspect of our lives, whether it be personal or professional, we encounter diversity in various forms. And it is through the recognition and celebration of this diversity that we can truly foster growth, understanding, and innovation. In the workplace, prioritizing diversity is not only the morally right thing to do, but it also yields numerous benefits for any business.

The concept of diversity is expansive and includes any variations that exist among a group of individuals. It encompasses a wide range of characteristics, such as race, ethnicity, gender, age, disability, and more. However, it is essential to note that diversity extends beyond these visible aspects and also encompasses less apparent dimensions, including religious diversity and sexual orientation, among others.

Religious diversity is a vital component of any inclusive workplace. It involves the presence of different religions, beliefs, and practices within a team. Religion can profoundly shape an individual's values, behaviors, and perspectives, and thus has a significant impact on their interactions within the workplace. By fostering a workplace culture that respects and values religious diversity, organizations allow for a more open environment where different viewpoints thrive.

Respecting religious diversity involves being mindful of any unconscious biases. Employees should be knowledgeable about different religions and spiritual beliefs, showing respect and empathy towards their colleagues' practices and customs.

Sexual orientation is another essential dimension of diversity that should be considered in promoting inclusivity.

Sexual orientation refers to an individual's emotional and physical attraction towards others and their overall sense of identity. Creating a workplace where individuals feel comfortable expressing their sexual orientation without fear of discrimination is crucial for fostering diversity and inclusion.

The LGBTQIA+ community, which includes individuals who identify as lesbian, gay, bisexual, transgender, queer or questioning, intersex, asexual, and more, deserves recognition and support in the workplace.

This diverse community represents strength and solidarity in the face of adversity and discrimination. Companies must implement inclusive hiring strategies and ensure open communication lines and policies that protect LGBTQIA+ individuals. By providing a safe and welcoming environment, organizations can enable members of this community to thrive and contribute fully to the success of the business.

Prioritizing diversity, including religious diversity and sexual orientation, in the workplace has numerous benefits for any organization. Firstly, it provides access to a broader range of ideas, perspectives, and experiences, which can be invaluable in problem- solving and decision-making processes. By encouraging a diverse workforce, companies can tap into the collective creativity and intelligence of individuals from different backgrounds, leading to innovative solutions and improved operations. Moreover, diversity in the workplace boosts employee morale and engagement. When employees feel that their unique identities and perspectives are valued, they are more likely to be motivated, productive, and loyal. inclusivity fosters a sense of belonging and psychological safety, allowing individuals to bring their whole selves to work. This, in turn, leads to increased job satisfaction, reduced turnover rates, and a more positive and supportive work environment.

Furthermore, prioritizing diversity in the workplace enhances a company's reputation. In today's globally connected world, consumers are increasingly conscious of an organization's values and commitment to social responsibility. By embracing diversity, businesses can attract a wider customer base and create stronger relationships with their stakeholders.

Diversity in all its forms is a powerful force that shapes our personal and professional interactions. Within the workplace, the prioritization of diversity, including religious diversity and sexual orientation, yields numerous benefits for any business.

By creating an inclusive culture that values and celebrates the differences among employees, companies can access new ideas and unique perspectives, improve overall operations, boost employee morale and engagement, and enhance their reputation. In our diverse world, embracing and embracing diversity is not just the right thing to do; it is an essential driver of success and growth for organizations.

Here are some steps companies can take to ensure employees feel safe and supported in expressing their sexual orientation in the workplace:

1. **Implement and enforce non-discrimination policies:** Companies should have clear policies that explicitly state non-discrimination based on sexual orientation and gender identity. These policies should be widely communicated and reiterated regularly to all employees.

2. **Provide LGBTQ+ sensitivity training:** Conduct training sessions or workshops to educate employees on LGBTQ+ issues, terminology, and respectful communication. This helps create awareness and promotes a more inclusive work environment.

3. **Foster an inclusive culture:** Create an inclusive culture that celebrates diversity and actively promotes LGBTQ+ inclusivity. Encourage employee resource groups or support networks where LGBTQ+ employees can connect and seek support within the organization.

4. **Harassment prevention and reporting mechanisms:** Establish a robust system for reporting discrimination, harassment, or bullying incidents. Ensure employees know how to report such incidents and provide multiple channels (such as anonymous reporting) to ensure their safety and confidentiality

5. **Support employee resource groups:** Encourage the formation of LGBTQ+ employee resource groups and provide them with adequate funding, resources, and support from leadership. These groups can advocate for LGBTQ+ issues, organize events, and provide a safe space for dialogue and support.

6. **Review and revise benefits and policies:** Evaluate existing benefits and policies to ensure they are inclusive of LGBTQ+ employees and their partners or families. This may include healthcare coverage, parental leave policies, and other benefits that support diverse family structures.

7. **Lead by example:** Senior leadership should openly endorse diversity, inclusion, and LGBTQ + rights within the workplace. Leaders should actively support initiatives and participate in events that promote inclusivity to set the tone for the entire organization.

8. **Allyship program s:** Encourage and support the formation of allyship programs where employees can pledge support and demonstrate solidarity with the LGBTQ+ community. Offer training and resources to help employees become better allies.

9. **Evaluate and address unconscious bias:** Regularly evaluate recruitment, promotion, and evaluation processes to identify and address any unconscious biases that may exist. This helps ensure that decisions are made solely based on merit and not influenced by prejudices.

10. **Celebrate diversity:** Celebrate cultural diversity and LGBTQ + milestones and events throughout the year. This can help normalize LGBTQ+ identities and contribute to an inclusive work environment.

It is important to note that these steps alone may not be sufficient, and organizations should regularly assess their efforts, solicit feedback from employees, and adapt their strategies accordingly.

Sexual orientation refers to a person's enduring pattern of emotional, romantic, and sexual attractions towards others. It is a fundamental aspect of one's identity, shaping their relationships, experiences, and sense of self.

While society often simplifies sexual orientation into categories like heterosexual, homosexual, or bisexual, the reality is far more complex and diverse.

This Section explores the different types of sexual orientation, including asexual, homosexual, heterosexual, bisexual, and pansexual, highlighting the importance of acknowledging and respecting this rich spectrum of human experiences.

Asexual individuals experience a lack of attraction, whether emotional, sexual, or romantic, towards others. This does not mean that they are incapable of forming deep and meaningful relationships; rather, their connections with others may be based on friendship, companionship, or platonic love. Understanding and accepting asexual individuals is crucial in a society that often centers sexuality as a defining characteristic of human relationships.

Homosexual individuals have an attraction towards people of the same sex. This orientation challenges traditional societal norms and often faces prejudice and discrimination. However, society is progressively becoming more accepting and understanding of same-sex relationships. Love and attraction do not discriminate based on gender, and it is vital that we continue to champion equal rights and respect for all individuals, regardless of their sexual orientation.

On the opposite end of the spectrum, heterosexual individuals experience an attraction towards people of the opposite sex. This is the most commonly recognized sexual orientation, and it often goes unchallenged in society.

However, it is important to recognize that heterosexuality is just one of the many valid ways in which people can experience attraction and love. By promoting inclusivity and diversity, we can foster a more tolerant and accepting world for all sexual orientations.

Bisexuality refers to individuals who experience an attraction towards both sexes. This orientation challenges the notion of a binary understanding of sexuality, acknowledging that attraction is not limited to one gender. Bisexual individuals may face unique challenges, such as stereotypes, invisibility, or even discrimination within both heterosexual and homosexual communities. It is crucial for society to recognize and respect bisexuality as a valid and authentic sexual orientation.

Pansexuality is another sexual orientation that often gets overlooked or misunderstood. Pansexual individuals experience an attraction towards any human being, focusing on qualities and personalities rather than gender. This orientation emphasizes that love and attraction are not confined to traditional gender norms, but rather exist on a spectrum that encompasses all human beings. By embracing pansexuality, we broaden our understanding of human relationships and challenge. societal norms that prioritize gender as the sole determinant of attraction.

It is essential to recognize and value the diverse range of sexual orientations that exist in society. By doing so, we promote inclusivity, respect, and equality for all individuals, regardless of their gender identity or sexual orientation.

It is not the responsibility of any individual to conform to societal expectations or to fit into a predetermined category. Rather, it is society's responsibility to create an environment that acknowledges and respects the diversity of human experiences.

I conclude that sexual orientation encompasses a broad spectrum of human experiences. Asexual, homosexual, heterosexual, bisexual, and pansexual orientations all contribute to the rich tapestry of human sexuality.

Recognizing, respecting, and accepting these diverse sexual orientations is essential for fostering a more inclusive and tolerant society. Through education, understanding, and empathy, we can create a world where everyone is free to express their authentic selves and love whomever they choose.

Gender Diversity

Gender diversity refers to the range of identities and expressions that go beyond traditional male and female roles. It recognizes that there are individuals who do not fit into the binary categories of male or female, and may identify as transgender, non- binary, or genderqueer, among others.

Gender diversity is an important aspect of workplace diversity as it challenges traditional gender norms and promotes inclusivity for all employees.

Creating a gender-inclusive workplace starts with addressing the biases and stereotypes that exist around gender. It is crucial for employers to provide equal opportunities and ensure that all voices are heard, regardless of gender identity.

This can be achieved through inclusive language and policies, such as gender- neutral restrooms and dress codes, as well as providing support for employees who are undergoing gender transition.

By embracing gender diversity, businesses can benefit from a broader array of perspectives and experiences. It can lead to more innovative and creative problem- solving, as well as increased employee satisfaction and retention. Additionally, having a gender-diverse workforce can help companies better understand and cater to the needs and preferences of a wider range of customers and clients.

Ethnic and Cultural Diversity

Ethnic and cultural diversity encompasses the variety of backgrounds, traditions, and beliefs that individuals bring to the workplace. It includes differences in race, ethnicity, nationality, language, and cultural practices. Embracing ethnic and cultural diversity can lead to a more enriched and dynamic work environment.

Having a diverse workforce allows for the exchange of different perspectives, ideas, and approaches to problem-solving. It helps to break down cultural barriers and fosters a sense of understanding and respect among employees. By valuing and celebrating different cultures, companies can create a more inclusive workplace that promotes collaboration and mutual learning.

Ethnic and cultural diversity also play a crucial role in reaching and connecting with diverse customer bases. Companies that understand and appreciate the cultural needs and preferences of their customers are more likely to succeed in today's global and multicultural marketplace. It allows for the development of products and services that cater to a wider range of customers, leading to increased customer satisfaction and loyalty.

Age Diversity

Age diversity refers to the range of ages present in the workplace, from younger generations to older generations. It recognizes that individuals of different age groups bring unique perspectives, experiences, and skills to the table. Embracing age diversity is important for creating a well- rounded and inclusive workplace.

By having a diverse age range in the workforce, companies can benefit from a mix of fresh ideas, enthusiasm, and technological prowess from younger employees, as well as the wisdom, experience, and stability of older employees.

This diversity can lead to more innovative problem-solving, increased productivity, and overall organizational success.

Age diversity also helps companies better understand and connect with different demographic groups, particularly in industries that cater to specific age ranges, such as fashion, technology, or healthcare.

It promotes a holistic approach to business operations and decision-making, taking into consideration the needs and preferences of various age groups. As diversity is a multifaceted and essential aspect of any workplace.

Whether it is religious, sexual orientation, gender, ethnic and cultural, or age diversity, it brings a wide range of perspectives, experiences, and ideas to the table. Embracing diversity in the workplace not only promotes inclusivity and equality, but it also enhances overall organizational
performance and success.

Companies that prioritize diversity are more likely to attract top talent, retain valuable employees, and appeal to a wider customer base. It fosters a culture of acceptance, collaboration, and creativity, leading to improved problem-solving and increased innovation. By embracing diversity, businesses can create a stronger and more resilient workforce that thrives in a rapidly changing and interconnected world.

Creating a culture of inclusivity and support

Creating a culture of inclusivity and support for employees with different sexual orientations requires a proactive and comprehensive approach to create an environment where everyone feels valued and included.

Here are some ways in which companies can promote such a culture:

1. **Implement non-discrimination policies:** Companies should establish clear policies that explicitly prohibit discrimination based on sexual orientation. These policies should be communicated to all employees and strictly enforced.

2. **Educate and train employees:** Conduct diversity and inclusion training programs to raise awareness and understanding about different sexual orientations, LGBTQ+ issue s, and the importance of creating an inclusive workplace. This training should be provided at all levels of the organization.

3. **Provide leadership support:** Senior leaders should publicly support diversity and inclusion initiatives and actively seek to create an inclusive culture. This includes vocalizing their commitment to supportingemployeesofall sexualorientationsand leadingbyexample.

4. **Foster employee resource groups:** Establish and support employee resource groups (ERGs) or affinity groups for LGBTQ+ employees. These groups provide a platform for employees to interact, share experiences, and provide support.

5. **Review and update HR policies:** Regularly review and update HR policies, such as anti-harassment and anti-discrimination policies, to ensurethey are inclusive and considerate of all sexual orientations. **NOTE: All Policies should take into account transgender employees as well**

6. **Make healthcare benefits inclusive:** Ensure that employer-provided healthcare benefits cover the medical needs of LGBTQ+ employees, including transitioning-related procedures, hormone therapy, mental health, and sexual health services.

7. **Provide inclusive facilities:** Create gender-neutral restrooms and make suitable modifications to facilities to accommodate the needs of transgender employees. This can help ensure an inclusive and safe workplace for all employees.

8. **Promote LGBTQ+ representation:** Encourage LGBTQ + representation in marketing materials, leadership positions, and public events. **This shows a commitment to diversity.**

9. Foster Allyship programs: Encourage employees to become allies by establishing allyship programs or mentorship initiatives[2.7] Allie s can provide support and advocacy for LGBTQ+ employees, helping create a more inclusive and supportive environment.

10. Celebrate LGBTQ+ events: Recognize and celebrate important LGBTQ+ events such as Pride Month and National Coming Out Day. This can involve organizing events, displaying symbols of support, and promoting awareness within the company.

11. Review recruitment and hiring practices: Review the recruitment and hiring process to ensure that it is inclusive and doesn't discriminate against candidates based on sexual orientation. Train recruiters and hiring managers to evaluate candidates based on skills, qualifications, and cultural fit, not sexual orientation. Remember that creating a culture of inclusivity and support is an ongoing process. Regularly assess the effectiveness of initiatives, gather feedback from employees, and make necessary adjustments to ensure continuous improvement.

Creating a culture of inclusivity and support for employees with different sexual orientations requires a proactive and comprehensive approach to create an environment where everyone feels valued and included.

Remember that creating a culture of inclusivity and support is an ongoing process. Regularly assess the effectiveness of initiatives, gather feedback from employees, and make necessary adjustments to ensure continuous improvement.

It's crucial for companies to continuously evaluate and update their practices to create an inclusive work environment for employees with different sexual orientations. Open and ongoing communication with employees is key to understanding their needs and challenges to create meaningful change.

Multiculturalism in the Workplace

Multiculturalism in the workplace refers to the acceptance, appreciation, and integration of individuals from diverse cultural backgrounds. Today, organizations all over the world are recognizing the importance of embracing cultural diversity in order to improve work performance, foster innovation, and promote a harmonious work environment.

As we look at the significance of multiculturalism in the workplace, including its benefits and challenges, as well as strategies that can be adopted to effectively manage and leverage cultural diversity.

One of the primary benefits of multiculturalism in the workplace is its potential to enhance creativity and innovation. Studies have shown that diverse teams tend to generate more ideas and solutions compared to homogeneous teams.

When individuals from different cultural backgrounds come together, they bring with them unique perspectives, ideas, and experiences. This diversity of thought, coupled with open communication and collaboration, enables organizations to tackle complex problems from multiple angles, leading to more innovative solutions.

Moreover, embracing multiculturalism in the workplace also improves cross-cultural awareness and understanding. As employees interact with colleagues from different backgrounds, they become more knowledgeable about different cultures, traditions, and customs.

This increased cultural competency fosters mutual respect, empathy, and the breakdown of stereotypes. By promoting a safe and inclusive work environment, multiculturalism contributes to job satisfaction and employee morale, leading to higher productivity and lower turnover rates.

However, multiculturalism in the workplace does present certain challenges that organizations need to address. One of the key challenges is effective communication. Language barriers, differing communication styles, and non-verbal cues can hinder collaboration and understanding among team members.

Organizations must invest in language training programs and encourage diverse employees to actively participate in cultural exchange activities to bridge communication gaps. Another challenge is the potential for unconscious bias and discrimination. Stereotyping and prejudice against individuals from certain cultural backgrounds can undermine the benefits of multiculturalism.

To address this, organizations need to implement robust diversity and inclusion policies, develop training programs on bias awareness, and establish zero-tolerance policies for any form of discrimination or harassment. By actively promoting inclusivity and equal opportunities, organizations can create a culture where employees feel valued, respected, and motivated to contribute their best.

Managing cultural diversity in the workplace also requires effective leadership and teamwork. Managers need to foster an environment of trust, respect, and open dialogue where everyone's opinions are valued.

It is crucial to create opportunities for employees to engage in cross-cultural collaboration, team-building activities, and intercultural training. This will help break down barriers, enhance understanding, and promote a sense of unity among diverse team members.

Multiculturalism in the workplace offers numerous benefits for organizations in today's globalized world. It promotes creativity, enhances cross-cultural awareness, and improves employee satisfaction. However, managing cultural diversity effectively requires addressing challenges such as communication barriers, unconscious bias, and discrimination. By implementing inclusive policies, providing cultural awareness training, and fostering open dialogue, organizations can create an environment that celebrates diversity and leverages it as a strength.

Multiculturalism in the workplace is not just about meeting legal requirements or meeting diversity quotas; it is about embracing the full range of perspectives and experiences that individuals from diverse cultural backgrounds bring, ultimately leading to increased innovation, productivity, and success in organizations

Sexual Orientation

Sexual orientation plays a significant role in the workplace, as it is an inherent aspect of an individual's identity and can greatly impact their overall experience and well-being. The workplace is a space where individuals should feel respected, supported, and valued, regardless of their sexual orientation.

In this section we will explore the importance of creating an inclusive and non- discriminatory environment for individuals of diverse sexual orientations, the benefits of doing so, and the challenges that persist. Firstly, it is crucial for organizations to embrace diversity and inclusivity by implementing policies that prohibit discrimination based on sexual orientation. By doing so, companies communicate their commitment to providing a safe and discrimination-free environment for all employees.

Such policies also send a positive signal to potential recruits, indicating that the company values diversity and promotes equality. This, in turn, opens the doors to a wider pool of talent, enabling organizations to attract and retain highly skilled individuals from various backgrounds. Moreover, creating an inclusive workplace environment for individuals of diverse sexual orientations fosters a sense of belonging and supports better mental health and overall well-being. When employees feel comfortable and accepted for who they are, they are more likely to be engaged and motivated, leading to increased productivity.

Conversely, an environment that is hostile or discriminatory can lead to diminished mental health, higher stress levels, and lower job satisfaction, ultimately affecting employee performance and retention.

Recognizing and addressing the unique challenges faced by employees with diverse sexual orientations is another integral aspect of creating an inclusive workplace. While progress has been made in recent years, discrimination and bias still persist, albeit in more subtle forms. Stereotypes and implicit biases can affect hiring decisions, promotions, and access to career opportunities. LGBTQ+ individuals may also be reluctant to share their personal lives at work due to fear of judgment or potential negative consequences.

Organizations can combat these challenges by fostering a culture of acceptance, promoting education and awareness through diversity training programs, and encouraging open dialogue. LGBTQ + employee resource groups or support networks can provide a safe space for employees to connect, share experiences, and access resources.

By creating these networks, organizations demonstrate their commitment to supporting their workforce's diverse needs, ultimately contributing to a sense of inclusion and belonging. Legal protections against discrimination based on sexual orientation also play a vital role in ensuring equal opportunities in the workplace. Many countries have enacted legislation that protects individuals from being discriminated against on the basis of their sexual orientation.

However, it is essential to ensure these legal protections are effectively enforced and accompanied by robust mechanisms for reporting and addressing instances of discrimination. Additionally, organizations should go beyond compliance with legal requirements and actively advocate for LGBTQ + rights and equality.

Sexual orientation is an intrinsic aspect of an individual's identity and should not be a factor that determines their treatment or opportunities in the workplace.

Creating an inclusive environment that is free from discrimination and bias benefits both employees and organizations. It fosters a sense of belonging, supports mental health and well-being, attracts diverse talent, and enhances productivity and employee satisfaction.

By actively promoting diversity, advocating for LGBTQ+ rights, and implementing policies that protect against discrimination, organizations can create a workplace that values and respects individuals' sexual orientations. A refresher on Sexual Orientation in the Workplace

The workplace, a setting where individuals spend a significant portion of their adult lives, should ideally be inclusive and respectful of all employees, regardless of their sexual orientation. Sexual orientation refers to an individual's enduring emotional, romantic, or sexual attraction to individuals of the same, opposite, or both sexes.

Understanding and acknowledging the different types of sexual orientation in the workplace is crucial for fostering a supportive environment, promoting diversity, and ultimately enhancing productivity.

Firstly, there is heterosexuality, which refers to individuals who are attracted to members of the opposite sex. Heterosexual employees comprise the majority of the population, and their sexual orientation has historically been assumed and privileged. However, it is essential to acknowledge that heterosexuality should not be the normative standard, but rather just one of the various sexual orientations present in the workplace. Valuing and accepting heterosexual individuals should be done alongside respecting and understanding individuals with different orientations, creating a more inclusive environment for all.

On the other end of the spectrum, there is homosexuality, referring to individuals who are attracted to members of the same sex. Homosexual employees often face unique challenges related to their sexual orientation in the workplace.

Discrimination and homophobia can manifest in various forms, such as exclusion from social activities, unequal treatment, or derogatory comments. To overcome this, employers need to cultivate a culture that promotes acceptance and discourages any form of discrimination based on sexual orientation.

This can be achieved through awareness campaigns, diversity training, and implementing policies that protect LGBTQ+ employees from harassment or discrimination.

Bisexual employees may face misconceptions, stereotypes, and stigma in the workplace. Some may assume that being attracted to both sexes means an inability to commit or decide on a sexual orientation, reinforcing harmful stereotypes.

It is crucial to raise awareness about bisexuality to foster a more supportive environment and to educate colleagues on what it means to be bisexual. Acknowledging and embracing bisexuality will ensure that employees can exist comfortably in an inclusive and accepting workplace.

As I shared previously, Pansexuality is another sexual orientation that is gaining recognition and visibility. Pansexual individuals are attracted to people regardless of their sex or gender identity. In the workplace, pansexual employees may experience misunderstanding or erasure due to the relatively recent recognition of this orientation.

It is essential for employers and colleagues to strive for inclusivity by educating themselves on pansexuality and acknowledging the validity of individuals' personal experiences. Additionally, asexual individuals experience little to no sexual attraction towards others. Instead of focusing on sexual relationships, they may prioritize emotional or intellectual connections. It is essential to acknowledge that asexuality is a valid sexual orientation and not merely a phase or a result of trauma. Asexuality can be an isolating experience, as it deviates from societal norms that emphasize sexual relationships. Promoting inclusivity and understanding asexuality is important, so asexual employees can feel comfortable and supported in the workplace.

Lastly, Employees who identify as queer may feel more comfortable with a fluid concept of their sexual orientation, wherein it is subject to change over time. Non-binary individuals may not exclusively identify as either male or female, and their sexual orientation can be diverse.

Understanding the various types of sexual orientations in the workplace is crucial for creating an inclusive and supportive environment. When we adjust our lenses, recognizing and respecting heterosexuality, homosexuality, bisexuality, pansexuality, asexuality, and other forms of sexual orientation promotes diversity, equality, and productivity. Employers must actively combat discrimination, provide education and training, and foster an environment that values every employee's unique experiences. By accommodating and embracing sexual diversity, workplaces can become truly inclusive spaces where all employees feel safe, accepted, and empowered.

What steps can employers take to create a safe and supportive workplace for employees of various sexual orientations?

1. **Develop and communicate a comprehensive non-discrimination policy:** Organizations should have a clear and extensive policy that explicitly prohibits discrimination based on sexual orientation. This policy should be communicated to all employees, and mechanisms should be in place to ensure that it is properly enforced.

2. **Provide diversity and inclusion training:** Regular diversity and inclusion training sessions should be conducted to educate employees about the importance of creating an inclusive workplace.

3. **Continued support for employee resource groups (ERGs):** Providing continued support for ERGs that specifically cater to the needs of LGBTQ+ employees. These groups provide a platform for employees from diverse sexual orientations to network, share experiences, and advocate for a more inclusive workplace environment.

4. **Implement inclusive HR policies:** Review and update HR policies to ensure they are inclusive of employees of all sexual orientations. This includes policies related to anti- harassment, benefits, family leave, dress code, and use of pronouns.

5. Foster an open and respectful culture: Encourage open dialogue and create a safe space where employees can share their experiences, concerns, and ideas without fear of discrimination or harassment. Encourage managers and leaders to actively listen and take action on any concerns raised.

6. Publicly support LGBTQ+ causes: Show support for LGBTQ+ rights by actively participating in events, such as pride parades, or sponsoring LGBTQ+ organizations. This demonstrates the organization's commitment to creating an inclusive workplace and can help build trust with employees.

7. Seek input from LGBTQ+ employees: Engage with LGBTQ+ employees through regular surveys, focus groups, or anonymous feedback channels to understand their experiences and gather ideas on how to improve the workplace environment. Actively involve them in decision-making processes related to diversity and inclusion initiatives.

8. Monitor and address any incidents of discrimination or harassment: Establish a reporting mechanism and investigate all reports of discrimination or harassment promptly and impartially. Take appropriate actions to address such incidents, including disciplinary measures, if necessary, to signal that such behavior will not be tolerated.

9. Continuously educate and evolve: Regularly review and update workplace policies, practices, and training programs to ensure ongoing improvement in supporting diversity and inclusion. Stay current with best practices and industry trends to adapt the organization's approach as needed.

Remember, creating a safe and supportive workplace for employees of diverse sexual orientations requires ongoing commitment and effort.

"To be one, to be united is a great thing. But to respect the right to be different is maybe even greater."
                                    — **Bono**

Chapter Four:

Check your Blind Spot: Identifying Unconscious Biases

Bias is an inherent part of human nature. As social beings, we have an innate tendency to categorize and make assumptions about the people and things around us. However, the problem arises when these biases create divisions among individuals and social groups, leading to unfair treatment and discrimination.

Social biases, which can be based on factors such as religion, sex, or race, have a detrimental impact on both organizations and society as a whole. They can hinder the development of inclusive environments and perpetuate harmful social norms. Biases can manifest as conscious or unconscious thoughts and actions, with the latter often resulting in more extreme forms of discrimination, such as harassment and violence.

Unconscious bias, also known as implicit bias, refers to the automatic and unintentional assumptions and beliefs that individuals hold about others. These biases are influenced by our personal experiences and backgrounds, and they can have a significant impact on our perceptions and judgments.

The danger lies in the fact that unconscious biases often operate outside of our conscious awareness, making them more difficult to identify and challenge. They can lead us to develop preferences or rejections toward certain individuals or groups, even if these biases do not align with our conscious values.

Various types of unconscious bias exist, each with its own set of consequences. For example, conformity bias occurs when individuals feel compelled to conform to the opinions and behaviors of those around them, often out of a desire to fit in.

This bias can overshadow one's true beliefs and opinions, leading to a lack of authenticity and critical thinking. In the workplace, this can have detrimental effects on decision- making processes and hinder the development of diverse perspectives and ideas. Gender bias is another prevalent form of unconscious bias that affects both men and women. It involves favoring one gender over

another or holding prejudiced views against a particular gender. This bias can be seen in various aspects of life, such as pay gaps, promotion opportunities, and unequal treatment in the workplace.

These biases perpetuate gender inequalities and restrict opportunities for individuals based on their gender, rather than their qualifications or abilities. The halo effect is yet another unconscious bias that influences our perceptions and judgments. It occurs when we form a positive impression of someone based on one particular attribute or quality they possess. However, this positive view may over shadow other aspects of the individual's character, leading to a biased and incomplete understanding of their overall capabilities and qualities.

Ageism, or discrimination based on age, is another common form of bias that deserves attention. While it often affects older individuals, ageism can impact any age group. Society tends to associate certain traits and abilities with different age groups, leading to unfair treatment and limited opportunities for individuals who do not fit those stereotypes. This bias can result in age discrimination in the workplace, limiting older individuals' career advancement opportunities and undermining their contributions and expertise.

Affinity bias, also known as similarity bias, is a preference for individuals who share similar experiences, interests, or backgrounds. This bias can have a negative impact on organizations by affecting the hiring process and creating an unequal and homogenous workforce.

When individuals hire and promote based on shared experiences rather than qualifications and abilities, organizations miss out on diverse perspectives and ideas which can impede their growth and innovation.

Bias, whether conscious or unconscious, has profound effects on society. It creates divisions among individuals and social groups, perpetuating discrimination and excluding certain individuals from opportunities and resources. Organizations suffer from a lack of diversity and inclusivity when biases go unchecked, hindering growth, creativity, and innovation. Recognizing and challenging our biases is crucial for creating a more equitable and harmonious society. By actively working to address biases and foster inclusivity, we can build a future where individuals are valued for their abilities and qualities rather than being subjected to unfair assumptions and judgments.

Organizations suffer from a lack of diversity and inclusivity when biases go unchecked, hindering growth, creativity, and innovation. Recognizing and challenging our biases is crucial for creating a more equitable and harmonious society. By actively working to address biases and foster inclusivity, we can build a future where individuals are valued for their abilities and qualities rather than being subjected to unfair assumptions and judgments. Unconscious biases contribute to the creation of social divides and unfair treatment of individuals within society in several ways:

1. **Stereotyping:** Unconscious biases often lead to the development and reinforcement of stereotypes, which are oversimplified and generalized beliefs or assumptions about certain groups of people. These stereotypes can create divisions by promoting negative perceptions and expectations about certain social groups, leading to unfair treatment and discrimination.

2. **Prejudice:** Unconscious biases can fuel prejudice, which is a negative attitude or feeling towards individuals or groups based on their perceived characteristics. Prejudice can result in individuals being treated unfairly or differently due to their race, ethnicity, gender, sexuality, or other social identities

1. **Discrimination:** Unconscious biases can influence behavior and decision-making, leading to discriminatory practices. Biased attitudes, even if unintentional, can affect hiring choices, promotion opportunities, access to resources, and overall opportunities for marginalized individuals, thereby perpetuating social divides and limiting their advancement.

2. **Confirmation bias:** Unconscious biases can influence how information is processed and interpreted. Individuals often tend to confirm their preexisting beliefs and biases, seeking out information that supports their views while disregarding or dismissing contradictory evidence. This confirmation bias can reinforce social divides by perpetuating misconceptions and preventing individuals from challenging their biases.

3. **Microaggressions:** Unconscious biases can manifest in the form of microaggressions, which are subtle, everyday behaviors or comments that convey derogatory or demeaning messages towards specific social groups. These microaggressions can create an environment that perpetuates unfair treatment, causing harm and reinforcing social divisions.

4. **Implicit bias in decision-making:** Unconscious biases can influence decision- making processes in various domains, including education, criminal justice, healthcare, and employment. These biases can result in unequal treatment, such as harsher punishments, biased evaluations, or unequal access to services, perpetuating social divides and systemic inequalities.

Addressing unconscious biases and raising awareness about their impacts is crucial to promoting equality and fairness within society. This can be achieved through education, training, and creating inclusive environments that encourage individuals to challenge their biases and foster understanding and empathy.

Stereotypes are deeply ingrained in our society, perpetuating harmful beliefs and creating a divide between different social groups. They are quick generalizations and categorizations of people based on their race, gender, culture, or religion. The consequences of stereotypes can be far-reaching, leading to discrimination, prejudice, and even violence. However, stereotypes are learned behaviors that can be unlearned through reflection, redefining perspectives, and evaluating their origins.

Cultural stereotypes are widespread, with people assuming that individuals from certain countries are rude, lazy, or warm and welcoming. These generalizations affect how we interact with people from different cultures, missing out on the opportunity to build meaningful relationships and strengthen organizations. Racial stereotypes perpetuate the belief that a certain race is greedy, athletic, or superior to others.

This creates divisions and perpetuates unfair treatment based on race. Gender stereotypes are also common, with assumptions made about the ability of certain genders to drive, excel in sports, be intelligent, or be untidy. These stereotypes limit opportunities for individuals and reinforce unequal gender norms.

Religious stereotypes are another prevalent form of stereotyping, assuming that people who practice a particular religion are wise or naive. These stereotypes can lead to discrimination and prejudice against individuals based on their religious beliefs.

Prejudice is the negative attitude and o[38]pinion that arises from stereotypes. It is based on assumptions rather than actual experiences or reasoning. Prejudice occurs when people view differences in others as weaknesses, leading to resentment and unfair treatment.

Prejudiced individuals judge others without getting to know them on a deeper level, assuming that everyone within a particular group is the same. This mindset hinders the creation of interpersonal relationships and equal opportunities. Discrimination, on the other hand, is the unfair treatment or actions that arise from prejudice. It can manifest as biased decisions or direct behaviors towards individuals. Discrimination violates an individual's human rights and can occur in various settings, including the workplace.

Discrimination in the workplace can take many forms, such as between employees, between an employer and their employees, or during the hiring process. A lack of diversity, equity, inclusion, and belonging in the workplace often leads to discrimination. Anti-discrimination laws exist to protect employees from prejudicial treatment based on race, age, disability status, pregnancy, and other protected categories.

Without these laws and a commitment to inclusivity, discrimination can perpetuate a toxic work environment. Harassment is a form of discrimination that involves unwanted or unpleasant behavior. It encompasses a range of offensive behaviors that demean or humiliate an individual. Harassment creates a hostile, disrespectful, and intimidating environment that can be damaging to both individuals and organizations. It may be a single incident or persist over time.

Harassment can occur based on an individual's sex, race, disability, or age. Examples of workplace harassment include sexual harassment, verbal harassment, physical harassment, and psychological harassment.

Sexual harassment involves explicit or implicit sexual implications, while verbal harassment includes inappropriate language intended to cause psychological harm. Physical harassment may include attacks or destruction of property, and psychological harassment is characterized by emotional bullying and unethical behavior towards others.

Stereotypes are harmful beliefs that categorize individuals based on their race, gender, culture, or religion. These quick generalizations lead to discrimination, prejudice, and even violence. Prejudice arises from stereotypes and involves negative attitudes and opinions based on assumptions rather than actual experiences. Discrimination is the unfair treatment resulting from prejudice and violates an individual's human rights.

Harassment is a form of discrimination that involves unwanted or unpleasant behavior and creates a hostile environment. Overcoming stereotypes requires reflection, redefining perspectives, and evaluating their origins to create more inclusive and equitable society.

While stereotypes can vary depending on the cultural, regional, and social context, here are some common stereotypes that exist in society today:

1. **Gender stereotypes:** These stereotypes include beliefs about the roles and characteristics assigned to men and women. For example, men are often stereotyped as strong, rational, and independent, while women are stereotyped as emotional, nurturing, and submissive.

2. **Racial and ethnic stereotypes:** These stereotypes involve assumptions and generalizations about different races and ethnicities. Examples may include overly simplistic or negative beliefs, such as associating specific ethnic groups with criminal behavior or intelligence.

3. **Age stereotypes:** These stereotypes involve assumptions about people based on their age. For instance, older adults may be stereotyped as forgetful or incapable, while young people may be stereotyped as lazy or entitled.

4. **Religious stereotypes:** These stereotypes involve preconceived notions about different religious groups. For instance, some may stereotype Muslims as terrorists or associate negative traits with specific religious beliefs.

5. **LGBTQ+ stereotypes:** These stereotypes involve assumptions and generalizations about people based on their sexual orientation or gender identity. Examples include assuming that gay men are effeminate or that transgender individuals are mentally unstable.

6. **Disability stereotypes:** These stereotypes involve assumptions and generalizations about individuals with disabilities. For instance, people with physical disabilities may be stereotyped as weak or incapable, while those with mental disabilities may face stigmatization or treated as intellectually inferior.

It is important to note that stereotypes are often oversimplifications that do not reflect the diversity and individuality present within any group. Stereotyping can perpetuate biases, prejudice, and discrimination, creating barriers to understanding and inclusivity.

Stereotypes can have a significant impact on marginalized communities in society today. Here are some ways in which stereotypes affect these communities:

Reinforcement of Inequality: Stereotypes often perpetuate existing inequalities and discriminatory practices. These biases can lead to systemic disadvantages and hinder social progress by reinforcing negative beliefs and prejudices towards marginalized group.

Limited Opportunities: Stereotypes can restrict access to education, employment, healthcare, and other essential resources. Marginalized communities may face discrimination, bias, and lower expectations based on stereotypes, leading to limited professional growth and economic opportunities.

Negative Self-Image and Identity: Stereotypes can undermine the self- image, self-esteem, and sense of identity of individuals from marginalized communities. Constant exposure to negative stereotypes can contribute to internalized oppression, feelings of shame, and a loss of belonging within society.

Impact on Mental Health: The constant exposure to stereotypes and discrimination can have severe psychological consequences. Marginalized individuals may experience higher levels of stress, anxiety, depression, and trauma, resulting in mental health disparities within these communities.

Stereotype Threat: Stereotypes can create a "stereotype threat" where individuals perform poorly on tasks or tests due to the fear of confirming negative stereotypes associated with their marginalized group. This can hinder academic and professional achievements and perpetuate the cycle of inequality.

Misrepresentation in Media: Misrepresentation or underrepresentation in media perpetuates stereotypes and can further marginalize communities. It can lead to a lack of diverse narratives, limited representation of role models, and reinforce harmful stereotypes about beauty, intelligence, or cultural practices.

Unequal Treatment in Criminal Justice System: Stereotypes often influence the treatment of marginalized communities in the criminal justice system. They can result in biased policing, harsher sentences, and racial profiling, contributing to mass incarceration and perpetuating cycles of poverty within these communities. Addressing stereotypes is crucial to promoting social justice and equality. Education, raising awareness, and encouraging diverse representation can help challenge and break down these harmful biases.

Society is replete with stereotypes that often shape our perception of others. Stereotypes are widely-held beliefs or generalizations about a particular group, which tend to oversimplify or categorize individuals based on their social, cultural, or racial characteristics.

Although it is crucial to recognize that stereotypes are frequently inaccurate and unjust, they persist due to various factors such as media influence, ignorance, and personal biases. Several common stereotypes prevalent today include those related to race, gender, and occupation. Racial stereotypes are deeply ingrained in society and continue to perpetuate discrimination and inequalities.

For instance, the stereotype that African Americans are prone to criminal behavior persists despite extensive evidence to the contrary. This belief not only reinforces prejudice but also leads to racial profiling and unwarranted suspicion within law enforcement agencies.

Similarly, the stereotype that Asian individuals excel exclusively in math and science contributes to the perception that other skills and talents are undervalued within this community. Stereotypes associated with Hispanics as undocumented immigrants or criminals have resulted in negative attitudes towards this ethnic group, leading to the unjust treatment and unequal opportunities for Hispanics in various contexts.

Another prevalent stereotype exists regarding gender roles and expectations. Women have historically been subjected to the stereotype that they are weaker and less capable than men, resulting in societal disadvantages such as limited career opportunities and unequal pay.

Women who challenge this stereotype by pursuing leadership roles or expressing assertiveness may face backlash and be labeled as aggressive or difficult. On the other hand, men often face stereotypes that demand stoicism and discourage emotional expression, which can have detrimental effects on mental health and intimate relationships.

These stereotypes hinder individuals from embracing their unique capabilities and restrict society from benefiting from diverse perspectives and talents.

Occupational stereotypes also heavily influence how individuals are perceived in society. Some common examples include the belief that all lawyers are money- hungry and opportunistic, or that all artists are extremely emotional and unstable.

Such stereotypes limit people's understanding of the complexity and diversity within different professions and can lead to misunderstandings and prejudice. Additionally, they discourage individuals from pursuing their passions or entering fields in which they may genuinely excel due to the fear of being judged according to these preconceived notions.

The media plays a significant role in fostering and perpetuating stereotypes. Television shows, movies, and advertisements often rely on stereotypes to simplify and package characters and narratives, catering to quick and easily recognizable tropes.

For instance, women are often portrayed as overly emotional and dependent on men, reinforcing existing stereotypes about female behavior. Similarly, racial stereotypes are frequently depicted, such as the portrayal of certain ethnicities as exotic, dangerous, or intellectually inferior.

These portrayals not only reinforce stereotypes among viewers but can also shape the perceptions and beliefs of those who lack real-world exposure to diverse group.

Stereotypes also persist due to ignorance and personal biases. Limited exposure to different cultures and perspectives can lead individuals to form superficial judgments.

Stereotypes continue to exist in society today, contributing to discrimination, inequality, and misunderstandings. Common stereotypes related to race, gender, and occupation negatively impact individuals and hinder societal progress.

By recognizing the detrimental consequences of stereotypes, fostering cultural awareness, and challenging personal biases, we can work towards a more equitable and inclusive society. It is essential to remember that stereotypes do not define individuals; instead, embracing diversity and embracing complexity should be our guiding principles.

What we need to do is learn to respect and embrace our differences until our differences don't make a difference in how we are treated." - **Yolanda King**

Chapter Five:

Microaggressions on Full Display

In today's society, both unintentional and intentional behaviors and words can have harmful and long-term effects on individuals, making them feel as though they do not belong. These impactful actions and words, often referred to as microaggressions, are prevalent in various aspects of society, including the modern workplace. Microaggressions are based on stereotypes and stigmatizations of race, sexual orientation, gender, and other marginalized groups.

They take various forms and shapes, and unfortunately, they are often overlooked within organizations. However, it is crucial to recognize the reality of microaggressions in the workplace in order to foster a culture that supports diversity, inclusion, and equity. Microaggressions can range from seemingly harmless comments or actions to more overt discriminatory behavior. They are rooted in implicit biases that individuals hold and reflect the pervasive societal norms and prejudices.

For instance, an unintentional microaggression may involve someone making a comment that assumes all individuals belonging to a particular racial or ethnic group share the same characteristics or abilities. On the other hand, intentional microaggressions involve deliberate acts of discrimination or derogatory language, such as making offensive jokes or using slurs.

Regardless of intent, the impact of microaggressions can be deeply damaging. These subtle acts can create a negative working environment, where individuals from marginalized groups feel uncomfortable, demeaned, and insulted. When microaggressions are allowed to persist, they contribute to a hostile workplace culture that hampers productivity, increases employee turnover, and ultimately undermines the organization's ability to achieve its goals.

Often, microaggressions go unnoticed or unaddressed because they may seem insignificant or trivial to those who haven't experienced them firsthand. However, dismissing the impact of microaggressions only perpetuates the harmful power dynamics and exclusionary practices within an organization. Therefore, it is important for individuals and organizations to become aware of and educated about microaggressions, as well as their consequences.

Creating a workplace environment that is truly inclusive and supportive requires recognizing and actively combating microaggressions. Organizations can implement various strategies to address this issue. First and foremost, education and awareness training should be provided to all employees. This training should focus on recognizing, understanding, and addressing microaggressions, as well as promoting empathy, respect, and cultural sensitivity. Furthermore, fostering open communication and establishing channels for reporting incidents of microaggressions is crucial. Employees should feel safe and encouraged to speak up when they experience or witness discriminatory behavior. Organizations must ensure that such reports are taken seriously and prompt action is taken to address and resolve them. Additionally, leaders within the organization should take responsibility for creating an inclusive workplace culture by modeling respectful behavior and addressing instances of microaggressions when they occur. They can establish diversity and inclusion committees or task forces to continuously evaluate and improve the organization's practices.

Organizational policies and procedures should also explicitly address microaggressions and provide guidelines on appropriate behavior. This includes setting clear consequences for engaging in discriminatory behavior and establishing support systems for individuals who have been subjected to microaggressions.

Unintentional and intentional behaviors and words can perpetuate harmful microaggressions that have long-term effects on individuals and undermine a culture of diversity, inclusion, and equity in the workplace.

Recognizing the reality of microaggressions is a critical step towards creating a more inclusive and encouraging environment. By educating employees, fostering open communication, and implementing supportive policies, organizations can strive towards eliminating microaggressions and ensuring that everyone feels valued and respected.

Only through such concerted efforts can organizations truly harness the power and potential of a diverse workforce.

What are Microaggressions?

Microaggressions are a pervasive and damaging form of discrimination that occurs on a daily basis in various social settings. These insults, snubs, or actions are meant to negatively target individuals or groups belonging to marginalized communities based on attributes such as race, gender, sexual orientation, disability, or other protected characteristics. Although microaggressions may often be unintentional, they have a profound impact on the targeted individuals, contributing to feelings of marginalization, exclusion, and unworthiness.

Microaggressions can take many forms, ranging from seemingly innocent jokes, questions, or casual remarks, to more subtle nonverbal behaviors such as gestures or facial expressions. What sets microaggressions apart from overt acts of discrimination is their subtlety and frequency. While blatant acts of discrimination are easy to identify and condemn, microaggressions often go unnoticed or are dismissed as harmless. However, their cumulative effect can be just as harmful, if not more so, especially when individuals are repeatedly subjected to them.

One common characteristic of microaggressions is that they communicate derogatory feelings and hostility towards the targeted individual or group. These derogatory attitudes are often rooted in implicit biases held by the perpetrator, which may stem from societal stereotypes or cultural conditioning. It is essential to recognize that microaggressions do not require malicious intent to cause harm. Even a seemingly harmless comment can contribute to the internalized oppression and self-doubt experienced by marginalized individuals.

One common type of microaggression is the "compliment" that carries an underlying assumption of inferiority or exoticization. For example, a common microaggression towards people of Asian descent is the assumption that they are good at math or possess unique cultural knowledge. While on the surface this may seem like a positive stereotype or compliment, it perpetuates the notion that individuals from marginalized communities are valuable only when they conform to preconceived notions or stereotypes.

Another form of microaggression is invalidation, where the experiences and perspectives of marginalized individuals are dismissed or trivialized. For example, questioning the legitimacy of someone's gender identity or sexual orientation by asking invasive questions or implying that it is just a phase, erases the lived experiences and struggles of LGBTQ+ individuals.

These invalidating comments not only contribute to feelings of invisibility and isolation but also perpetuate harmful stereotypes and prejudices. Microaggressions are not isolated incidents but occur within a broader context of systemic racism, sexism, homophobia, and other oppressive structures. The effects of microaggressions can accumulate over time, leading to heightened stress, anxiety, depression, and self- esteem issues.

Research has shown that experiencing chronic microaggressions is associated with adverse physical and mental health outcomes, including cardiovascular problems, increased cortisol levels, and decreased overall well- being. Moreover, microaggressions can have far-reaching consequences on a societal level. They have the power to perpetuate and reinforce existing power imbalances, further marginalizing and excluding already oppressed groups.

When we participate in or begin the process of knowing or unknowingly normalizing discriminatory behavior, microaggressions inhibit progress towards achieving true equality and social justice. Addressing microaggressions requires a multi-faceted approach that includes education, awareness, and active allyship. It is crucial for individuals to examine their own biases and assumptions and engage in self-reflection to become more aware of their own microaggressive behaviors.

Education and awareness campaigns can play a significant role in increasing and empathy, enabling individuals to recognize and challenge microaggressions when they occur. Being an ally involves actively advocating for marginalized individuals, listening to their experiences, and speaking out against discriminatory practices. Microaggressions are harmful acts of discrimination that occur in everyday life, often unintentionally and subtly.

These insults, snubs, and actions target marginalized individuals or groups based on attributes such as race, gender, sexual orientation, or disability. While they may not always be malicious in intent, microaggressions can have serious and long-lasting effects on the well-being and self-esteem of the targeted individuals. Recognizing and challenging microaggressions is essential for fostering an inclusive and equitable society that respects the dignity and worth of all individuals, regardless of their background or identity.

Recognizing and addressing microaggressions in interpersonal interactions requires both self-awareness and effective communication skills.

Here are some strategies and techniques to consider:

Practice self-care: Addressing microaggressions can be emotionally draining. Take care of yourself and seek support from friends, allies, or support groups. Engaging in self-care allows you to recharge and continue advocating against microaggressions.

Educate yourself: Familiarize yourself with common forms of microaggressions and their impact by reading books, articles, and resources on the subject. This knowledge will enable you to recognize microaggressions when they occur.

Reflect on your own biases: Be aware of your own implicit biases and stereotypes. Engage in self-reflection to understand how your beliefs and actions might unintentionally perpetuate microaggressions.

Active listening: Pay attention to others' experiences and perspectives. Practice active listening to understand and empathize with the impact of microaggressions on marginalized individuals.

Call it out when appropriate: In a respectful and non-confrontational way, address the microaggression when you witness one. Use "I" statements to express how it made you feel and why it is problematic. For example, "I felt uncomfortable when you made that comment. It perpetuates stereotypes and can be hurtful."

Focus on the behavior, not the person: Separate the microaggression from the individual. Rather than attacking the person's character, focus on the specific behavior or comment that was problematic. This allows for a more constructive conversation.

Provide education and feedback: Offer information and resources to help the person understand the impact of their words or actions. Share informative articles, books, or documentaries that provide diverse perspectives and knowledge.

Be patient and open to dialogue: Recognize that change takes time. Some individuals may be unaware of their microaggressions or defensive when confronted. Be patient and engage in open dialogue to provide them with opportunities for growth and learning.

Remember, it is crucial to approach these conversations with empathy, understanding, and a willingness to learn from one another. Addressing microaggressions in the moment can be challenging, but it is crucial for maintaining a productive and inclusive conversation.

Here are some effective ways to approach this:

1. **Be self-aware:** Recognize your own biases and assumptions before addressing someone else's microaggressions. This will help you approach the   situation with empathy and understanding.

2. **Stay calm and composed:** Responding with anger or defensiveness may escalate the situation. Take a deep breath and respond in a calm and collected manner.

3. **Assume good intentions:** Give the person the benefit of the doubt and assume that they may be unaware of the impact of their words or actions. Approach the conversation with the intention of educating or raising awareness, rather than accusing or attacking.

4. **Use "I" statements:** Express how their comment made you feel, using "I" statements. For example, "When you said that, I felt uncomfortable because it perpetuates a harmful stereotype."

5. **Ask clarifying questions:** Seek clarity by asking open-ended questions to encourage reflection. This can help the person realize the microaggression and its impact. For example, "What did you mean by that?" or "Could you expand on your statement?"

6. **Share personal experiences:** If you feel comfortable, you can share your personal experiences to help the person understand the impact of their words or actions. Personal stories can be powerful and foster empathy.

a. **Educate rather than attack:** Explain why the comment or behavior is considered a microaggression, highlighting its impact and the underlying stereotypes or biases. Share resources or suggest further reading to deepen their understanding

b. **Encourage dialogue:** Foster an open conversation by inviting the person to share their perspective. This dialogue can expand awareness and promote mutual understanding.

c. **Maintain respect:** Be respectful and open-minded throughout the conversation, even if the other person becomes defensive or dismissive. Remember that change takes time and patience.

d. **Seek support:** If the conversation becomes too challenging or the person is resistant to your attempts, consider seeking support from a mediator or discussing it with someone you trust. Not every conversation will result in immediate change, but planting a seed of awareness can have a long-term impact.

e. **Choose the right time and place:** Addressing microaggressions in private, one- on-one conversations is often more effective than calling someone out in public. This allows for a more relaxed environment where defensiveness is less likely to arise. Remember, addressing microaggressions requires patience, understanding, and a commitment to fostering inclusive conversations.

The goal is to bring awareness and understanding to promote change rather than provoking defensiveness or hostility. However, it's important to note that some people might still respond defensively even when approached tactfully. In such situations, it is crucial to prioritize your emotional well-being and determine if continuing the conversation is productive or necessary.

The Main Categories of Microaggressions

Microaggressions are subtle, everyday actions or comments that may seem harmless to the perpetrator but have a negative impact on the recipient, particularly those from marginalized groups. Coined by psychiatrist Chester M. Pierce in the 1970s, microaggressions can be seen as a form of indirect discrimination, perpetuating stereotypes and reinforcing power imbalances. While microaggressions can manifest In various forms, they can be broadly categorized into three main categories: microassaults, microinsults, and microinvalidations.

1.   **Microassaults** are the most overt category of microaggressions. They are purposeful and explicit actions or comments that are intended to degrade or offend someone based on their marginalized identity.

Usually, microassaults are consciously discriminatory and reflect explicit prejudices and biases. For example, using racial slurs or making derogatory comments about someone's sexual orientation are forms of microassaults.

Such acts are often more easily recognizable as discriminatory and are therefore more likely to be challenged directly. However, this category of microaggression also includes more covert actions, such as intentionally excluding someone from a social event due to their race or gender.

2.   **Microinsults** are more subtle forms of microaggressions that are often unintentional but still carry a harmful message. They are usually rooted in implicit biases and can manifest through seemingly innocent comments or actions that demean a person's identity.

These acts may indicate that the perpetrator holds stereotypes or prejudices without explicitly expressing them. An example of a microinsult would be asking a person of Asian descent, "Where are you really from?" implying that they do not truly belong in the country.

Similarly, making assumptions about someone's intelligence or abilities based on their race or gender can also be considered a microinsult. Although microinsults are less explicit than microassaults, their cumulative effect can lead to a hostile environment and contribute to the ongoing marginalization of certain groups.

3. **Microinvalidations** are microaggressions that undermine, delegitimize, or negate someone's experiences or identity. They often deny the existence of systemic oppression or dismiss personal perspectives, minimizing the concerns and lived experiences of marginalized individuals.

Microinvalidations can take the form of denying the impact of racism, sexism, or other forms of discrimination, suggesting that a person is being too sensitive, or attributing their achievements solely to their gender or race. For example, telling someone, "You're so articulate for a Black person," implies an underlying expectation that Black individuals are less intelligent or well-spoken. These acts of invalidation can be deeply damaging, as they deny the very existence of oppression and invalidate the emotions and experiences of those affected by it.

It is important to note that microaggressions can occur across a wide range of identities, including race, gender, sexual orientation, disability, and more. They can affect individuals both directly and indirectly, perpetuating stereotypes, and reinforcing systemic inequalities. The impact of microaggressions should not be underestimated, as they can erode an individual's self-esteem, contribute to a hostile environment, and reinforce power dynamics.

Addressing microaggressions requires a multifaceted approach. Education and awareness are crucial for both perpetrators and bystanders. By recognizing and acknowledging one's own biases and the potential harm caused by microaggressions, individuals can actively work towards creating a more inclusive and equitable environment. Additionally, creating safe spaces for marginalized individuals to share their experiences and providing platforms for empowerment and dialogue are essential in addressing the effects of microaggressions.

Microaggressions can be categorized into three main categories:

Microassaults, Microinsults, and Microinvalidations. Each category manifests in different ways, from explicit acts of discrimination to more subtle forms of demeaning comments or actions. Recognizing and understanding the impact of microaggressions is crucial in dismantling systemic inequalities and creating a more inclusive society.

Through education, awareness, and active intervention, we can work towards eradicating microaggressions and fostering an environment that values and respects the diverse experiences and identities of all individuals.

The Harm caused by *Microaggressions*

Microaggressions are subtle, everyday exchanges that can have profound negative effects on individuals from marginalized groups. These seemingly innocent comments, actions, or gestures can cause harm and stress to the targeted individual, affecting them mentally, emotionally, and even physically. Despite their small size, microaggressions have macro effects, reinforcing ideas that contribute to the isolation and social exclusion of particular groups, perpetuating inequality and discrimination in society.

One of the most significant harms caused by microaggressions is their detrimental impact on an individual's mental health. Constant exposure to microaggressions can lead to feelings of confusion, hopelessness, fear, anxiety, and anger.

These emotions can build up and result in chronic stress, which has been linked to various mental health issues such as depression, anxiety disorders, and even suicidal ideation. The cumulative effect of microaggressions over time can significantly impact an individual's self-esteem and overall well-being.

Moreover, microaggressions can also affect an individual's emotional health and sense of belonging in their community or workplace. These subtle acts of discrimination can create an environment of alienation and invalidation, making it difficult for individuals to feel accepted and valued.

The constant subtle slights and dismissals can erode an individual's confidence and sense of worth, leading to feelings of self-doubt and isolation.

In the workplace, the impact of microaggressions can be particularly harmful. Constant exposure to microaggressions can create a hostile work environment for individuals in marginalized groups, hindering their ability to perform their job effectively.

The stress and emotional toll caused by these acts can decrease job satisfaction and motivation, leading to lower work productivity and performance. Furthermore, microaggressions can also discourage individuals from marginalized groups from striving for promotions or applying for job opportunities. The fear of facing continued discrimination can discourage them from seeking advancement and limit their career progression, perpetuating inequality in the workplace.

The harm caused by microaggressions extends beyond the individual level. These acts of exclusion perpetuate systemic inequalities and discrimination in society. By reinforcing stereotypes and biases, microaggressions contribute to the marginalization of particular groups, hindering their access to resources, opportunities, and social networks. The subtle and pervasive nature of microaggressions allows them to go largely unnoticed, making it challenging to address and combat these harmful behaviors effectively.

To mitigate the harm caused by microaggressions, it is crucial to raise awareness and promote education about the effects of these subtle acts of discrimination. Individuals should be trained to recognize and understand microaggressions, fostering a culture of inclusion and respect. Organizations need to establish clear policies against discrimination, including microaggressions, and provide channels for reporting and addressing such incidents.

It is essential to challenge societal norms and beliefs that contribute to the devaluation and marginalization of specific groups. This requires ongoing efforts to promote diversity and inclusion, ensuring that all individuals have an equal opportunity to thrive and succeed.

Microaggressions, despite their subtle nature, can have profound negative effects on individuals from marginalized groups. The harm caused by microaggressions extends beyond the individual level, perpetuating discrimination and inequality in society. The cumulative impact on mental health, emotional well-being, and work performance can be significant. Intentionally Recognizing, addressing, and eradicating microaggressions is crucial for promoting a more inclusive and equitable society.

Experiencing frequent microaggressions in a workplace or academic setting can have several potential consequences for the individuals involved.

Here are some of them:

1. **Psychological impact:** Frequent exposure to microaggressions can lead to increased stress, anxiety, and emotional distress. It may contribute to feelings of frustration, anger, self-doubt, and diminished self-esteem. Over time, these effects can negatively impact mental health and overall well-being.

2. **Reduced productivity and engagement:** Constant exposure to microaggressions can hinder an individual's ability to focus, concentrate, and perform at their best. It may lead to decreased motivation, reduced job satisfaction, and disengagement from work or academic pursuits, ultimately affecting productivity and achievement.

3. **Decreased sense of belonging:** Microaggressions can create an unwelcoming and exclusionary environment. Individuals who experience them may feel alienated, marginalized, or like they do not fit in within the workplace or academic community. This diminished sense of belonging can negatively impact their relationships with colleagues, peers, and supervisors, as well as their overall job or academic satisfaction.

4. **Impaired professional and academic growth:** Frequent microaggressions can impede an individual's professional or academic progress. It may limit opportunities for advancement, networking, mentorship, and collaborative projects. The cumulative effect of microaggressions can hinder career or educational development, potentially leading to missed opportunities and reduced long-term success.

5.   **Physical health impact:** The stress caused by experiencing microaggressions can have physical manifestations such as headaches, muscle tension, sleep disturbances, and weakened immune system response. Over time, this may increase the risk of developing various health issues and negatively impact overall well-being.

6.   **Influence on career choices:** The experience of frequent microaggressions may influence an individual's career decisions. It could lead them to avoid certain industries, workplaces, or academic fields that are known to have a higher prevalence of such behaviors. This self-selection process might limit opportunities or further exacerbate existing inequalities within certain sectors.

It is important to acknowledge that the impact of microaggressions is highly individual and context-dependent. People may respond differently, and the consequences can vary based on factors such as personal resilience, available support systems, organizational culture, and the severity of these incidents.

How to Respond to Microaggressions

Microaggressions are subtle, often unintentional acts or comments that convey insensitive or discriminatory messages towards marginalized groups. While they may seem insignificant to some, they can cause significant harm and erode trust and inclusivity in the workplace. To address microaggressions effectively, both the receiver and perpetrator must take specific steps to foster a positive company culture that values diversity and equality.

For individuals who have experienced microaggressions, responding proactively is essential. One of the most effective ways to address microaggressions is to speak up and be direct when they occur. By calmly and assertively explaining to the perpetrator how their behavior or comment negatively impacts you, you can increase their awareness and potentially open a broader discussion on the topic.

This approach not only educates the perpetrator but also empowers the individual to assert their rights and express their feelings.

It is crucial for those who experience microaggressions not to internalize them. Internalizing such incidents can lead to feelings of self-doubt, diminished self- worth, and even psychological distress. Instead, the focus should be on immediately countering the microaggression by responding promptly and firmly. Using "I" statements to address the perpetrator, such as "I felt hurt when you said/ did ... " allows for clear communication and helps the perpetrator understand the impact of their message.

To address microaggressions effectively, it is important to separate the intent of the message from its impact. While the perpetrator may not have intended to cause harm, the impact is what matters most. By shifting the focus of the conversation from their intent to the effect of their words, individuals can foster empathy and open up a dialogue that leads to understanding and growth.

Taking care of oneself is equally crucial when dealing with microaggressions. The emotional toll of constantly encountering such incidents can be draining. It is essential to find healthy ways to process these experiences, whether by confiding in a trusted friend, seeking support from a professional therapist, or engaging in self-care practices. By nurturing one's mental and emotional well-being, individuals can maintain resilience and continue to advocate for change.

For those who have communicated a microaggression, listening and understanding the concerns of the individual affected is the first step towards growth and change.

It is essential to provide a safe space for them to express their feelings, and to express gratitude for their willingness to bring the issue to your attention. Acknowledging their concerns and apologizing sincerely for the impact of your message is crucial. It demonstrates a genuine effort to rectify the harm caused and rebuild trust.

In responding to microaggressions, it is important not to make the situation about oneself. It is natural to feel defensive when confronted with one's own biases, but it is crucial to resist this defensive tendency. Instead, focus on the impact of your actions and avoid attempting to explain or rationalize them.

Acknowledge that you may have unknowingly contributed to the marginalization of a group and take responsibility for your actions.

To prevent future occurrences of microaggressions, one must actively seek awareness and knowledge. It is important to educate oneself about the experiences and struggles of marginalized groups, and to constantly challenge one's preconceptions. By reading literature, attending workshops, or engaging in conversations with diverse individuals, one can develop a deeper understanding of the complexities of social identity and inequality. This active pursuit of education and awareness is essential for growth and for preventing future microaggressions.

Responding to microaggressions requires a collective effort from both the receiver and perpetrator. By speaking up and being direct, individuals can address microaggressions and educate perpetrators on their impact. Internalizing microaggressions should be avoided, and "I" statements can help express one's feelings. It is important to separate intent from impact and focus on the latter.

Taking care of oneself and seeking support is crucial for anyone's resilience. For perpetrators, listening, acknowledging, and apologizing sincerely are key steps in rectifying the harm caused. It is important not to make the situation about oneself and to take responsibility for the impact. Seeking awareness and knowledge is important for preventing future microaggressions.

By fostering a positive company culture that values diversity and equality, microaggressions can be minimized, and workplaces can become more inclusive and empowering for all.

"Leadership should be focused on extending the ladder of opportunity for everyone."

Justin Trudeau

Chapter Six:

Communication, Lifting Every Voice

Communication is a fundamental aspect of human interaction, enabling us to convey thoughts, ideas, and emotions to others. It can take various forms, including verbal and non-verbal, and differs among individuals based on their backgrounds and experiences. Effective communication plays a crucial role in fostering Diversity, Equity, Inclusion, and Belonging (DEIB) as it helps create a sense of understanding, respect, and acceptance among diverse individuals.

To communicate effectively, we need to go beyond simply comprehending others' words; we must also ensure that they feel heard and valued. This is particularly important when communicating with individuals from culturally diverse backgrounds, as their perspectives and experiences may differ significantly from our own. By being sensitive and mindful of these differences, we can create an inclusive environment where everyone feels welcome to contribute and share their voice.

Inclusive communication involves adapting our language and approach to accommodate the needs and preferences of our audience. It requires us to consider the ways in which others may receive and interpret our messages. For instance, individuals from different cultural backgrounds may have varying levels of proficiency in the language we are using. To ensure effective communication, we should aim to use accessible language, avoiding jargon or complex terminology that might confuse or alienate certain individuals.

Additionally, when communicating with a culturally diverse audience, it is crucial to be aware of potential cultural nuances and differences in communication styles. For example, direct, assertive communication may be highly valued in some cultures, while others may prioritize indirect and harmonious communication. By recognizing and respecting these cultural variations, we can promote understanding and avoid unintentionally causing offense or misunderstanding.

Alongside verbal communication, non-verbal cues such as facial expressions, gestures, and body language play a significant role in conveying meaning. However, it is important to note that these cues can also vary across cultures. For instance, maintaining direct eye contact during a conversation is considered a sign of attentiveness and respect in some cultures, while in others, it may be seen as confrontational or disrespectful. By being mindful of these differences, we can adjust our non-verbal communication to create a more inclusive and comfortable environment for all individuals.

Furthermore, effective communication within the context of DEIB involves actively listening to and valuing the perspectives of others. It requires open-mindedness and a willingness to engage in constructive dialogue. By actively seeking out diverse voices and opinions, we can expand our understanding of different experiences, fostering a sense of belonging for all individuals within the discourse.

Communication is a two-way process that necessitates both speaking and listening. In the pursuit of DEIB, it is essential to create spaces that encourage individuals to share their perspectives without fear of judgment or exclusion. By promoting inclusivity and actively encouraging participation from all individuals, we can create an environment where everyone feels comfortable expressing their thoughts and ideas. This not only leads to a richer and more diverse range of perspectives but also enhances collaboration, problem-solving, and innovation.

Effective communication is a vital component of DEIB. By adapting our language, being sensitive to cultural nuances, and actively listening to diverse perspectives, we can create an inclusive environment where every voice is lifted. Through inclusive communication, we promote understanding, respect, and a sense of belonging, fostering stronger relationships and enabling individuals to reach their full potential. As we continue to strive for DEIB, it is essential to recognize that communication is the key that unlocks the door to a more inclusive and equitable society.

Effective communication can play a crucial role in fostering Diversity, Equity, Inclusion, and Belonging (DEIB) in a culturally diverse setting by:

Creating an open and inclusive environment: Effective communication ensures that everyone has a voice and feels encouraged to share their perspectives and experiences. It allows individuals from different backgrounds and cultures to express themselves and contribute to discussions.

Encouraging empathy and understanding: Good communication facilitates active listening, empathy, and understanding of others' viewpoints. It helps individuals comprehend and appreciate different cultural backgrounds, experiences, and perspectives, promoting a more inclusive and tolerant culture.

Breaking down barriers and stereotypes: Effective communication helps dismantle stereotypes by encouraging dialogue and the exchange of ideas. By showcasing diverse thoughts and perspectives, it challenges preconceived notions and fosters a more inclusive mindset.

Encouraging collaboration and teamwork: Strong communication skills facilitate effective collaboration within diverse teams. Open and transparent communication helps build trust, encourages cooperative problem-solving, and supports innovative thinking through the blending of different viewpoints.

Promoting equity and fairness: Effective communication ensures that information, opportunities, and resources are accessible to all. It helps in establishing clear expectations, providing feedback, and recognizing individual contributions, promoting a fair and equitable environment for all individuals.

Addressing conflicts and resolving misunderstandings: Culturally diverse settings may sometimes lead to misunderstandings or conflicts. Effective communication enables open and honest dialogue, helping resolve conflicts constructively and encouraging shared understanding.

Enhancing belonging and engagement: When individuals feel seen, heard, and valued, they are more likely to feel a sense of belonging and engagement. Effective communication practices, such as active listening, providing constructive feedback, and recognizing accomplishments, contribute to creating an inclusive culture that fosters a sense of belonging for all individuals.

Overall, effective communication serves as a foundation for creating an inclusive environment that values diversity, promotes equity, embraces different perspectives, and fosters a sense of belonging for all individuals in a culturally diverse setting.

So, how does effective cross-cultural communication contribute to breaking down barriers and stereotypes, fostering greater understanding and appreciation for diversity amidst a culturally diverse group?

Effective cross-cultural communication plays a crucial role in breaking down barriers and stereotypes and fostering greater understanding and appreciation for diversity in a culturally diverse group.

Here are some ways how it contributes to these goals:

1. **Promotes empathy and perspective-taking:** Cross-cultural communication allows individuals to view the world from different cultural lenses, enabling them to develop empathy and understanding of others' perspectives. This understanding helps to break down preconceived notions and stereotypes, as individuals gain a more nuanced and accurate understanding of different cultures.

2. **Enhances awareness of cultural differences and similarities:** Through effective communication, individuals become aware of the diverse values, customs, and practices of different cultures. This awareness helps to challenge stereotypes by highlighting the complexities and variations within cultures, reducing generalizations and misunderstandings.

3. **Builds trust and rapport:** Effective cross-cultural communication involves active listening, respect, and open-mindedness. When individuals feel respected and understood, trust is built, and barriers are broken down. Developing trust and rapport among culturally diverse groups paves the way for increased collaboration, cooperation, and appreciation for diversity.

4. **Encourages learning and education:** Effective cross-cultural communication allows for the sharing of knowledge, experiences, and insights. It promotes a learning environment where individuals can ask questions, seek clarification, and engage in meaningful conversations, leading to a greater understanding of diverse cultures. This learning aspect helps dispel stereotypes and contributes to a more well-rounded perception of different cultures.

5. **Encourages inclusive decision-making:** In a culturally diverse group, effective cross-cultural communication ensures that everyone's voices are heard and considered. This inclusivity helps break down barriers and stereotypes by challenging dominant cultural norms or biases that may exist within the group, fostering a more equitable and diverse decision-making process.

6. **Develops cultural competence:** Effective cross-cultural communication allows individuals to develop cultural competence, which is the ability to interact and communicate effectively with people from different cultural backgrounds. By learning about others' cultures, individuals become more sensitive to cultural differences and adapt their communication styles accordingly. This competence contributes to better understanding and appreciation of diversity.

Overall, effective cross-cultural communication is a catalyst for breaking down barriers and stereotypes within culturally diverse groups by promoting empathy, increasing awareness, building trust, encouraging learning, fostering inclusivity, and developing cultural competence. It facilitates a more inclusive and respectful environment that appreciates and embraces diversity. Diversity is an ever-present reality in today's globalized world, with individuals from different cultural backgrounds, races, religions, and ethnicities coming together in various settings, such as workplaces, educational institutions, and communities.

While diversity brings numerous benefits, it also presents challenges in the realm of communication. Communication barriers arising from diversity can impede understanding, collaboration, and relationships between individuals from different backgrounds. In this essay, we will explore some of the key diversity communication barriers and their significance.

One of the fundamental diversity communication barriers is language. Language is not only a means of expressing thoughts and ideas but also an integral part of one's culture and identity. It is important to understand that when individuals from different linguistic backgrounds interact, language barriers can hinder effective communication. Misunderstandings, misinterpretations, and even conflicts may arise due to language barriers.

For instance, slang words or idiomatic expressions may not have equivalent translations in other languages, leading to confusion or even offense. Moreover, differences in pronunciation or accents can make it difficult for people to understand each other clearly.

Language barriers can limit opportunities for collaboration and hinder the sharing of ideas and knowledge among diverse groups.

Cultural differences also play a significant role in diversity communication barriers. Each culture has its unique set of values, beliefs, norms, and customs that influence communication styles. For example, in some cultures, direct and assertive communication is valued, while in others, indirect and subtle communication is preferred.

When individuals from different cultural backgrounds communicate, these differences in communication style can lead to misunderstandings and misinterpretations. Direct communicators may perceive subtle messages as dishonest or unclear, while indirect communicators may find direct communication as confrontational or rude.

Cultural differences can create barriers to building trust, understanding intentions, and resolving conflicts, ultimate ultimately hindering effective communication and collaboration. Moreover, communication can also contribute to diversity communication barriers to Diversity, Equity, Inclusion, and Belonging.

Non-verbal cues such as facial expressions, gestures, and body language are essential elements of communication, often complementing verbal messages. However, certain non-verbal cues can be misinterpreted or have different meanings across cultures. For instance, a nod of the head might be considered as agreement or understanding in one culture but perceived as disagreement or confusion in another.

Similarly, eye contact, touch, personal space, and physical gestures may carry different cultural connotations. As a result, individuals with different cultural backgrounds may misinterpret non-verbal cues, leading to confusion or misunderstandings in communication. Stereotypes and prejudices significantly impact diversity communication. Stereotypes are oversimplified and generalized beliefs about a particular group or individual, while prejudices involve preconceived judgments based on these beliefs.

Stereotypes and prejudices create barriers in communication by distorting perceptions and engendering biased attitudes. When people hold stereotypes or prejudices, they may make assumptions These assumptions can result in biased interpretations, discriminatory behaviors, and exclusion. about others' abilities, intentions, or values based on their cultural background.

Overcoming stereotypes and prejudices is crucial in fostering inclusive communication that allows for genuine empathy and understanding. Diversity communication barriers arise from various factors such as language differences, cultural disparities, non-verbal misinterpretations, and stereotypes. These barriers hinder effective communication and can lead to misunderstandings, conflicts, and limited collaboration between individuals from different backgrounds. It is essential to recognize and understand these barriers to promote inclusivity, empathy, and effective communication across diverse settings.

By valuing diversity, actively learning about different cultures, and adopting inclusive communication practices, individuals can bridge these communication barriers and create environments that celebrate diversity and promote mutual understanding.

Diversity is an ever-present reality in today's globalized world, with individuals from different cultural backgrounds, races, religions, and ethnicities coming together in various settings, such as workplaces, educational institutions, and communities. While diversity brings numerous benefits, it also presents challenges in the realm of communication.

Communication barriers arising from diversity can impede understanding, collaboration, and relationships between individuals from [61]different backgrounds.

We will explore some of the key diversity communication barriers and their significance. One of the fundamental diversity communication barriers is language.

Language is not only a means of expressing thoughts and ideas but also an integral part of one's culture and identity. When individuals from different linguistic backgrounds interact, language barriers can hinder effective communication. Misunderstandings, misinterpretations, and even conflicts may arise due to language barriers.

For instance, slang words or idiomatic expressions may not have equivalent translations in other languages, leading to confusion or even offense. Moreover, differences in pronunciation or accents can make it difficult for people to understand each other clearly. Language barriers can limit opportunities for collaboration and hinder the sharing of ideas and knowledge among diverse groups.

Cultural differences also play a significant role in diversity communication barriers. Each culture has its unique set of values, beliefs, norms, and customs that influence communication styles. For example, in some cultures, direct and assertive communication is valued, while in others, indirect and subtle communication is preferred.

When individuals from different cultural backgrounds communicate, these differences in communication style can lead to misunderstandings and misinterpretations. Direct communicators may perceive subtle messages as dishonest or unclear, while indirect communicators may find direct communication as confrontational or rude.

For instance, the nodding of the head that was shared earlier might be considered as agreement or understanding in one culture but perceived as disagreement or confusion in another. Similarly, eye contact, touch, personal space, and physical gestures may carry different cultural connotations. As a result, individuals with different cultural backgrounds may misinterpret non-verbal cues, leading to confusion or misunderstandings in communication.

Stereotypes and prejudices significantly impact diversity communication. Stereotypes are oversimplified and generalized beliefs about a particular group or individual, while prejudices involve preconceived judgments based on these beliefs.

Stereotypes and prejudices create barriers in communication by distorting perceptions and engendering biased attitudes. When people hold stereotypes or prejudices, they may make assumptions about others' abilities, intentions, or values based on their cultural background.

These assumptions can result in biased interpretations, discriminatory behaviors, and exclusion. Overcoming stereotypes and prejudices is crucial in fostering inclusive communication that allows for genuine empathy and understanding.

Diversity communication barriers arise from various factors such as language differences, cultural disparities, non-verbal misinterpretations, and stereotypes. **Diversity Communication Barriers** are often present and show up unannounced in our personal and professional lives. We must be able to recognize and address them head on through knowledge, skills, and awareness with courage.

The PCIHO Model

The objective of the PCIHO Model is to create an AWARENESS in individuals that they play a role in the organization's Diversity, Equity, Inclusion, and Belonging culture and to help them to self-identify their role.

PCIHO Framework - Questions to Consider:

1. As it relates to Diversity and Inclusion, how do you see your role in the organization?

2. Why do you believe that is the role you are playing on your team?

3. Is there another role you would like to play or aspire to play out on your team?

Pioneer

Champion

Influencer

Hesitator

Obstructor

email: jharris@chedufoundation.org to learn more about the PCIHO Model

Diversity Communication Barriers: Breaking Down the 5 Basic Objections Effective communication is the cornerstone of any successful organization or society. However, when it comes to diversity, there are often communication barriers that hinder understanding and collaboration. These barriers hinder effective communication and can lead to misunderstandings, conflicts, and limited collaboration between individuals from different backgrounds. It is essential to recognize and understand these barriers to promote inclusivity, empathy, and effective communication across diverse settings.

These barriers can arise from various factors, including cultural differences, language proficiency, unconscious bias, stereotypes, and the fear of being judged or misunderstood.

By using the **5 Basic Objections framework,** we can identify and address these barriers to build more inclusive and effective communication channels in diverse environments.

Objection 1: Cultural Differences

One of the primary obstacles to effective communication in diverse settings is cultural differences. Cultures vary significantly in terms of values, beliefs, customs, and communication norms. These differences can lead to misunderstandings and misinterpretations. For example, direct communication may be valued in one culture, while another culture highly values indirect communication.

To overcome this objection, it is crucial to promote cultural competence and awareness through education and training. Encouraging individuals to develop a genuine curiosity and respect for other cultures can foster better understanding and reduce miscommunication.

Objection 2: Language Proficiency

Language proficiency disparity is a common challenge faced in diverse communication settings. When individuals are not fluent in the dominant language or share a common language, effective communication becomes daunting. This can lead to exclusion, frustration, and misunderstanding

To address this barrier, organizations should invest in language support programs that provide language training and interpretation services. Additionally, encouraging openness and patience in communication can create a safe space for non-native speakers to express themselves without fear of judgment or ridicule.

Objection 3: Unconscious Bias

Unconscious bias is an often-overlooked barrier to effective diversity communication. We hold biases ingrained through upbringing, societal influences, and personal experiences. These biases can affect our perceptions and judgments, leading to unfair treatment or misunderstandings. Recognizing and confronting unconscious bias requires self-reflection and personal growth. It is crucial to create a culture of inclusivity and sensitivity, where all individuals are encouraged to challenge their own biases and actively listen to others without preconceived notions.

Objection 4: Stereotypes

Stereotypes are deeply ingrained assumptions about particular groups of people. These stereotypes can influence communication by leading to generalizations and assumptions that hinder understanding and cooperation. Overcoming stereotypes requires education, exposure, and firsthand experiences. Organizations can create diversity programs that encourage individuals to engage with people from different backgrounds, challenging preconceived notions and fostering empathy. By valuing individual stories and recognizing the uniqueness of each person, we can break down stereotypes and promote more effective communication.

Objection 5: Fear of Misjudgment

Fear of being misunderstood or judged can significantly impede communication in diverse settings. This fear arises from the lack of trust or misunderstanding of intentions. To tackle this barrier, it is crucial to establish an environment that encourages open dialogue, active listening, and empathy. Leaders should create safe spaces where individuals can express their thoughts and concerns without fear of retribution. Developing clear channels for feedback and ensuring anonymity can also help individuals feel secure in expressing their opinions.

Diversity communication barriers can be broken down by addressing the 5 Basic Objections to cultural differences, language proficiency, unconscious bias, stereotypes, and fear of misjudgment. By promoting cultural competence, investing in language support programs, challenging unconscious biases, addressing stereotypes, and fostering a safe and inclusive environment, organizations can cultivate effective communication channels in diverse settings.

Through these efforts, we can build bridges of understanding, nurture empathy, and promote collaboration among individuals from different backgrounds, ultimately leading to a more harmonious and inclusive society. Diversity communication barriers are obstacle s that arise due to difference s in culture, background, language, and perspective.

These barriers can hinder effective communication and create misunderstandings, biases, and conflicts in various settings, such as workplaces, educational institutions, and social gatherings.

We will explore the five basic objections framework to analyze the challenges that diversity communication barriers present and propose strategies to overcome them.

The first objection in the framework is ignorance, which refers to the lack of awareness or understanding of other cultures, norms, and values. Ignorance can lead to stereotypes, prejudice, and discrimination, thus impeding effective communication. For example, a person from one culture may unknowingly offend someone from a different culture by making comments or jokes that are considered disrespectful or insensitive in the other person's culture.

To overcome ignorance, individuals should engage in continuous learning and educate themselves about different cultures, customs, and perspectives. This can be done through attending cultural awareness workshops, reading diverse literature, or participating in intercultural exchanges. By actively seeking knowledge, individuals can broaden their understanding and enhance their ability to communicate respectfully and effectively with people from diverse backgrounds.

The second objection in the framework is insecurity, which stems from a fear of the unknown or an inability to handle differences. Insecure individuals may feel threatened by those who are different from them, leading to a defensive or hostile attitude. This can create a hostile environment for open and inclusive communication, as people may hesitate to express their true thoughts and opinions.

To address insecurity, fostering a safe and inclusive environment is crucial. This can be achieved by promoting diversity and inclusion initiatives within organizations and communities. By providing opportunities for open dialogue, encouraging collaboration, and celebrating diverse perspectives, people can feel more secure in expressing themselves and engaging in meaningful conversations. Additionally, cultivating empathy and practicing active listening can help individuals understand and respect different viewpoints, reducing the insecurity that often hinders effective communication.

The third objection is ego, which refers to a person's overvaluation of their own culture, beliefs, and ideas. Ego can lead to a lack of willingness to consider other perspectives and a tendency to dismiss or devalue different viewpoints. This can impede effective communication as it limits the exchange of ideas and stifles creativity and innovation.

To overcome ego, individuals should cultivate humility and develop a growth mindset. Recognizing that no single culture or perspective is superior can open doors for meaningful and inclusive communication. Actively seeking differing opinions, soliciting feedback, and encouraging diverse voices can help break down ego barriers and foster an environment that values and embraces diverse perspectives.

The fourth objection is control, which refers to individuals' desire to impose their own beliefs and expectations on others. Control can lead to micromanagement, the suppression of different ideas, and the stifling of individual expression. Such behavior creates a power imbalance and prevents effective communication from taking place.

To overcome control, individuals should practice delegation, empowerment, and inclusivity. By encouraging autonomy and shared decision-making, people can feel more empowered and valued, leading to improved communication and collaboration. Additionally, fostering a culture of respect and encouraging individuals to voice their opinions and challenge the status quo can facilitate open and honest communication.

The final objection is indifference, which occurs when individuals are apathetic towards diversity or marginalized groups. Indifference can result in exclusion, marginalization, and the perpetuation of stereotypes and discrimination. It hinders effective communication by creating divides between individuals and undermining trust and understanding.

To overcome indifference, promoting diversity and inclusion should be a priority. This can be achieved by creating diverse representation at all levels, providing equal opportunities for all individuals, and actively challenging and addressing bias and discrimination. By fostering an inclusive culture that values and celebrates diversity, individuals will be more inclined to engage in open and empathetic communication.

Diversity communication barriers pose significant challenges to effective communication. By acknowledging and addressing the objections of ignorance, insecurity, ego, control, and indifference, individuals and organizations can overcome these obstacles.

Cultivating awareness, empathy, and inclusivity are key strategies in breaking down these barriers and fostering a more inclusive and communicative society. Only then can we truly embrace the richness and strength that diversity brings to our lives.

1. Use a common language: Establish a common language that team members can use for communication. This can be English or any other mutually agreed-upon language that most team members understand.

2. Provide language training: Offer language training programs for team members who struggle with the common language. This can help them improve their language skills and enhance their ability to express themselves effectively.

3. Use visual aids: Utilize visual aids such as charts, diagrams, or presentations to supplement verbal communication. Visuals can provide a clearer understanding of concepts and facilitate communication across language differences.

4. Encourage active listening: Emphasize the importance of active listening in team interactions. Encourage team members to listen attentively to each other, ask for clarifications, and paraphrase to ensure understanding.

5. Simplify language: When communicating, try to use simple and clear language. Avoid using jargon, slang, or complex terminology that might confuse non-native speakers or those with limited language skills

6. Provide written documentation: Whenever possible, provide written documentation of important information, decisions, and instructions. This allows team members to review and refer back to the information at their own pace and can help clarify any misunderstandings.

7. Utilize technology: Leverage technology tools such as translation apps or software to bridge language gaps during conversations or written communication. These tools can aid in facilitating real-time translation, making it easier for team members to understand each other.

8. Foster a culture of respect and patience: Encourage team members to be patient and understanding with each other's language challenges. Cultivate a respectful and inclusive team culture that values diversity and supports open communication.

9. Use non-verbal communication: Non-verbal cues such as facial expressions, gestures, and body language can often convey meaning and emotion even without relying heavily on verbal communication. Encourage team members to use and interpret non-verbal cues to enhance understanding.

10. Develop team-building activities: Organize team-building activities that encourage interaction, cooperation, and understanding among diverse team members. These activities can help build relationships, trust, and improve cross- cultural communication.

Technology can be used to facilitate communication and overcome language barriers within a diverse team in several ways:

1. **Translation tools:** There are various online translation tools and apps that can instantly translate messages, emails, documents, and even conversations in real-time.

2. These tools make it easy for team members to communicate in their preferred language and quickly understand each other's messages.

3. **Video conferencing platforms:** Video conferencing platforms like Zoom, Microsoft Teams, or Google Meet provide features for live captioning and language interpretation, allowing participants to select their preferred language for real-time translation during meetings. This enables effective communication and understanding among team members who speak different languages.

4. **Collaboration tools:** Collaboration tools, such as project management software and document sharing platforms, can help overcome language barriers by providing features like multilingual interfaces, task assignment notifications, and comment translations. Team members can easily communicate and collaborate on projects, regardless of their language preferences.

5. **Language learning applications:** Language learning apps like Duolingo or Babbel can help team members learn basic phrases and words in different languages. This can enhance communication by allowing team members to have small conversations or understand common phrases, even if they don't speak each other's language fluently.

6. **Cultural awareness resources:** Technology can also provide access to cultural awareness resources, such as online courses, articles, or videos, which can facilitate understanding and bridge cultural gaps within a diverse team. A better understanding of each other's cultures can lead to improved communication and collaboration.

7. Instant messaging apps and chatbots: Instant messaging apps with built-in translation features, like WhatsApp or Slack, can enable real-time communication between team members who don't share a common language. Additional I y, chatbots programmed with multiple languages can assist with basic communication and provide instant translations when needed.

8. Virtual reality (VR) language training: Emerging technologies like virtual reality can simulate immersive language learning environments, where team members can practice speaking and listening to different languages within a safe and controlled virtual space. This can enhance language skills and improve communication within diverse teams.

By leveraging these technological solutions, diverse teams can overcome language barriers, foster effective communication, and create an inclusive and collaborative environment.

Chapter Seven:

The Illusion of Inclusive Leadership

The Illusion of Inclusive Leadership or "Illusion of Inclusion" refers to a situation where leaders, despite their claims of promoting diversity and inclusivity, fail to truly embrace and implement these values within their organizations. Oftentimes, this illusion is created when leaders focus on surface-level diversity metrics, such as gender or race, without truly addressing the systemic barriers and biases that prevent true inclusivity.

One common manifestation of the Illusion of Inclusive Leadership is tokenism. Leaders may appoint a diverse individual to a prominent position simply to meet diversity quotas or to improve the organization's image, without providing them with equal opportunities for growth and advancement. This creates a superficial appearance of inclusivity while maintaining the status quo of unequal power dynamics.

Additionally, leaders may resist challenging their own biases and perspectives, creating a culture where diverse viewpoints are not genuinely valued or considered. Inclusive leadership requires a willingness to listen, learn, and adapt, but leaders often fall into the trap of surrounding themselves with individuals who think and act like them, leading to a homogenous decision making process.

Another aspect of the Illusion of Inclusive Leadership is the lack of accountability for fostering an inclusive environment. Leaders may talk about the importance of inclusivity, but fail to hold themselves or others accountable for their actions and behaviors. Without clear expectations and consequences, inclusivity becomes a mere buzzword rather than a fundamental value.

To avoid falling into the trap of the Illusion of Inclusive Leadership, leaders must commit to self-- reflection and continuous learning. They must actively seek out diverse perspectives and ensure that all team members have equal opportunities for growth and development. It is crucial for leaders to cultivate an environment where all individuals feel safe, respected, and heard.

The Illusion of Inclusive Leadership can hinder the true progress towards diversity, equity, and inclusion within organizations. Leaders must go beyond superficial measures and actively work towards dismantling systemic barriers and biases. By fostering genuine connection, respect, and inclusivity, leaders can create an environment that drives innovation, problem-solving, and ultimately, organizational success. It is through consistent commitment, curiosity, and courage that leaders can break free from the Illusion of Inclusive Leadership and cultivate a truly inclusive culture.

The illusion of inclusive leadership can arise when leaders claim to embrace diversity and create an environment of inclusion, but fail to live up to these ideals in practice. It is one thing to say that diversity and inclusion are important, but it is another thing entirely to actively foster an inclusive environment.

First and foremost, inclusive leadership requires a commitment to diversity, equity, inclusion, and belonging. It is not enough for leaders to simply pay lip service to these concepts; they must truly believe in the value of diversity and actively work to cultivate an inclusive culture. This means ensuring that all team members are given equal opportunities to contribute and succeed, regardless of their race, gender, age, or background.

Inclusive leaders also exhibit curiosity, seeking to understand and learn from others' perspectives and experiences. This means actively seeking out diverse opinions and ideas, rather than surrounding themselves with like-minded individuals. By fostering an environment of curiosity, leaders can tap into the collective intelligence of their teams and make more informed decisions.

Perhaps most importantly, inclusive leadership requires courage. It takes courage to challenge the status quo, to question traditional norms and biases, and to stand up for what is right. Inclusive leaders must be willing to step outside their comfort zones and confront their own biases in order to create a truly inclusive environment. This may involve acknowledging and rectifying past mistakes or addressing instances of unconscious bias within the organization.

Inclusive leaders also understand the importance of creating a sense of connection and respect within their teams. They actively foster an environment where everyone feels valued and included, recognizing that diverse perspectives and backgrounds contribute to the overall success of the organization. This means creating opportunities for open dialogue and encouraging the sharing of ideas and experiences.

Inclusive leadership is not just a feel-good concept; it has tangible benefits for organizations. By embracing diversity and creating an inclusive environment, leaders can enhance problem-solving and decision-making processes. Different perspectives and experiences can lead to more innovative and effective solutions. Additionally, an inclusive culture can improve employee engagement, retention, and satisfaction, resulting in higher productivity and overall organizational success.

Despite the importance of inclusive leadership, there can be instances where leaders create an illusion of inclusivity. This can occur when leaders fail to follow through on their commitments, when diversity and inclusion become mere buzzwords without real action, or when leaders only embrace diversity for superficial reasons such as corporate image enhancement.

In these cases, the illusion of inclusion not only fails to achieve its intended goals, but it can also damage trust and hinder progress towards true inclusion. To avoid falling into the trap of the illusion of inclusive leadership, leaders must be self- aware and willing to examine their own biases and behaviors.

They must actively seek feedback from team members and be open to learning and growing. It is essential to hold leaders accountable for creating and maintaining an inclusive environment, ensuring that their words align with their actions.

Inclusive leadership is essential for organizations to thrive in a diverse and rapidly changing world. It requires commitment, curiosity, and courage from leaders. By fostering an environment of connection and respect, embracing diversity, and actively challenging biases, leaders can create a truly inclusive culture.

However, leaders must be careful to avoid the trap of the illusion of inclusive leadership, ensuring that their actions align with their professed values. Only through genuine and authentic inclusivity can organizations unlock the full potential of their diverse workforce and achieve sustainable success.

In the pursuit of building a diverse, equitable, and inclusive work environment, visible commitment plays a pivotal role. It requires a significant allocation of both energy and time, as well as an unwavering dedication to ensuring that diversity, equity, inclusion, and belonging (DEIB) are made a priority. Inclusive leadership lies at the core of this endeavor, driven by the values of fairness and the provision of equal opportunities for all.

An inclusive leader is committed to fostering a sense of belonging among employees, recognizing and understanding the unique needs of each team member. They acknowledge the responsibility that rests upon their shoulders to bring about powerful change, even if it means challenging established norms and holding individuals accountable.

One of the key ways in which inclusive leaders exhibit their commitment is by formulating a clear mission that encompasses everyone in the organization. This mission serves as a guiding principle for decision-making and emphasizes the importance of diversity, equity, inclusion, and belonging at all levels.

However, commitment must extend beyond mere words and intentions; it must be visible through actions.

Inclusive leaders actively recognize and address systemic biases and inequalities, making tangible strides towards creating a work environment where every individual feels valued and respected. Ultimately, visible commitment reflects an authentic dedication to DEIB. It requires leaders to continuously learn, adapt, and improve their strategies to ensure that the workplace is truly inclusive, fostering a culture of acceptance and equality. In the pursuit of building a diverse, equitable, and inclusive work environment, it is crucial for leaders to demonstrate visible commitment.

This visible commitment serves as a powerful catalyst for change, and is essential for fostering an environment where every individual feels valued, respected, and included. An inclusive leader is driven by their core values of fairness and equality of opportunity, and their commitment to these values guides their actions and decisions.

One of the fundamental aspects of visible commitment is making diversity, equity, inclusion, and belonging (DEIB) a priority. Inclusive leaders recognize that building an inclusive workplace requires deliberate effort and allocation of resources. They understand that it is not enough to simply pay lip service to these ideals, but rather, a comprehensive and sustained effort must be made to embed DEIB principles into the fabric of the organization. This involves dedicating time, energy, and resources to initiatives that promote diversity, address inequities, and foster a sense of belonging among employees.

An inclusive leader understands the importance of creating an environment where every team member feels a sense of belonging. They recognize that each individual has unique needs, and they take the time to understand and accommodate these needs. This involves actively listening to employees, seeking their input, and adapting policies and practices to ensure diversity and inclusion are embraced at all levels. By valuing each employee as an individual, inclusive leaders create an environmentwhere everyone feelsseen, heard, and appreciated.

Inclusive leaders also accept personal responsibility for creating powerful change. They understand that change begins at the individual level, and they are willing to challenge their own biases and assumptions. They actively seek out opportunities to educate themselves and engage in self-reflection, in order to deepen their understanding of the experiences and perspectives of others. This personal growth and self-awareness enable them to lead more effectively and dismantle systemic barriers that perpetuate inequalities.

Accountability is another key aspect of visible commitment. Inclusive leaders hold themselves and others accountable for their actions and behaviors. They do not shy away from addressing instances of bias, discrimination, or exclusion, and take appropriate actions to rectify the situation. By setting clear expectations and consequences for discriminatory behaviors, they foster a culture where everyone is responsible for upholding the principles of diversity, equity, and inclusion.

Visible commitment also requires challenging the status quo. Inclusive leaders are not afraid to challenge traditional norms and practices that perpetuate inequities. They actively seek out diverse perspectives and voices, and ensure that decision-making processes are inclusive and transparent.

By challenging the status quo, inclusive leaders create space for innovative ideas and

Inclusive leaders also recognize the importance of building on the ideas that others share. They understand that no one person has all the answers and that the best ideas often emerge through collaboration and group brainstorming.

By creating an environment where every individual is able to freely share their ideas, inclusive leaders encourage diverse thinking. They understand that diverse perspectives and experiences bring valuable insight and allow for a comprehensive examination of problems and opportunities.

Through inclusive leadership, employees are encouraged to challenge and question existing approaches, leading to continuous improvement and growth approaches that better reflect the needs and aspirations of all employees. A crucial component of visible commitment is the creation of a clear mission that incorporates everyone. Inclusive leaders articulate a compelling vision for the organization that is centered on diversity, equity, inclusion, and belonging. They communicate this vision consistently and authentically, and ensure that it is reflected in the organization's policies, practices, and strategic objectives. By aligning the entire organization around a shared mission, inclusive leaders create a sense of purpose and direction that inspires and motivates employees.

Visible commitment is integral to building a diverse, equitable, and inclusive work environment. Inclusive leaders prioritize DEIB, understand the unique needs of each team member, and hold themselves and others accountable. They challenge the status quo, continually educate themselves, and create a clear mission that incorporates everyone. An organization can only thrive when it truly values and embraces diversity, equity, inclusion, and belonging, and it is the visible commitment of its leaders that sets the tone for this transformation.

Empowering Others

Inclusive leaders seek to empower everyone by creating an environment in which every individual feels valued and able to contribute. They understand that successful collaboration requires input from all team members, as diverse thinking leads to innovative and effective solutions. These leaders foster an inclusive work environment where employees are encouraged to share their voices freely and participate in discussions and decision-making processes. In an inclusive work environment, employees feel a sense of empowerment. They are confident that their contributions are valued and that their perspectives are heard. This empowerment creates a sense of ownership and commitment to the team's goals and objectives. Employees are more likely to go above and beyond their assigned tasks, as they feel motivated and engaged.

Inclusive leaders understand that when individuals feel empowered, they are more likely to take risks and think creatively, ultimately leading to a more productive and successful team. However, inclusive leaders also understand that achieving diverse thinking requires more than just inviting everyone to the table. They recognize that some voices may be marginalized or unheard due to various reasons, such as cultural barriers, unequal power dynamics, or personal reservations. In such cases, inclusive leaders take active steps to ensure that these voices are included and heard.

They reach out to individuals who may be hesitant to contribute, provide opportunities for everyone to participate, and actively seek out and value diverse perspectives. By doing so, inclusive leaders create an atmosphere of trust and respect, making it easier for individuals to share their voices freely and confidently.

Another key aspect of inclusive leadership is fostering team cohesion. Inclusive leaders understand that in order to achieve successful collaboration, it is essential to build strong relationships within the team. They promote open communication, mutual trust, and respect among team members. By creating a positive and supportive team environment, inclusive leaders encourage everyone to actively participate, contribute, and learn from one another. They recognize the importance of both personal and professional growth and actively support and champion their team members' development.

One of the most important elements of inclusive leadership is the recognition that diverse thinking is crucial for effective collaboration. Inclusive leaders understand that diversity extends beyond visible differences such as race or gender. They appreciate the value of diverse perspectives, experiences, and backgrounds, and actively seek to include and leverage these differences in order to achieve better outcomes. By fostering an environment where diverse thinking is not only valued but actively sought after, inclusive leaders encourage creativity, innovation, and progress. Inclusive leaders seek to empower everyone by creating an environment in which every individual feels valued and able to contribute diverse thinking in effective collaboration and actively work towards including all voices.

Through empowering employees, encouraging diverse thinking, and fostering team cohesion, inclusive leaders create an atmosphere of trust, respect, and collaboration. They understand that by embracing and leveraging diversity, teams are better equipped to achieve their goals and strive for continued growth and success.

Cognizance of Bias

A signature trait of inclusive leadership is the cognizance of bias. In today's diverse and multicultural society, it is essential for leaders to recognize and address their own biases in order to create an inclusive and equitable environment. Biases are inherent in human nature, shaped by our upbringing, experiences, and societal influences. Inclusive leaders, however, demonstrate awareness and commitment towards understanding their personal and organizational biases.

Inclusive leaders do not hide or deny their biases; instead, they take responsibility and actively seek to challenge and change them. They acknowledge that biases can negatively impact decision-making, hiring practices, and team dynamics, leading to exclusion and discrimination. By recognizing their own biases, inclusive leaders are able to minimize their influence on judgment and behavior.

Self-awareness plays a crucial role in this process. Inclusive leaders must be introspective and willing to confront their own beliefs, attitudes, and preconceived notions. They take time to reflect on their own privileges and recognize that biases can be deeply ingrained. They seek feedback from others, actively listen to diverse perspectives, and encourage open dialogue. This not only helps them understand the impact of biases but also fosters a culture of inclusion and respect within their organizations. Furthermore, inclusive leaders are dedicated to continuous learning and growth. They educate themselves on different cultures, perspectives, and experiences, continually challenging their assumptions and expanding their knowledge. They actively seek diverse perspectives and experiences in decision-making processes, creating opportunities for marginalized voices to be heard and valued.

Inclusive leadership requires a conscious recognition of bias. Inclusive leaders are self-aware, committed to personal growth, and strive to create equitable and inclusive environments. By owning their biases and actively working towards change, inclusive leaders foster an environment where diversity is not only accepted but celebrated, benefiting not only individuals but also the organizations they lead.

Learning about and from Others

Curiosity is a fundamental aspect of human nature that enables personal growth and development. It cultivates an open mind, encourages diverse conversations, and fosters the exploration of new perspectives. Inclusive leaders, in particular, exemplify the power of curiosity by demonstrating a deep interest in others and their unique experiences.

Highly inclusive leaders understand the significance of embracing diverse opinions and actively seek out opportunities to engage in conversations with individuals from various backgrounds. They approach these interactions with an open mindset, free from preconceived notions or judgments. By listening attentively and refraining from making assumptions, inclusive leaders create a safe space for ideas to flourish and new insights to emerge.

An inclusive leader's curiosity allows them to better understand how others experience the world. This empathetic understanding helps them to not only acknowledge but also appreciate the perspectives of those different from themselves. Through respectful questioning and genuine interest, inclusive leaders foster an environment where individuals feel valued and represented.

Consequently, this promotes stronger connections and teamwork within a group or organization. Furthermore, curiosity expands our worldview and helps us challenge our biases. By actively seeking to understand lives different from our own, we gain a deeper appreciation for the richness and diversity of human experiences. With new perspectives, we can reframe our biases and broaden our understanding of the world, promoting empathy and inclusivity.

Curiosity is an essential catalyst for personal growth and development. It drives us to engage in diverse conversations, seek new perspectives, and challenge our biases. Inclusive leaders exemplify the power of curiosity, fostering a culture of understanding and empathy. By embracing curiosity, we can create a more inclusive society where every individual feels valued and represented.

Cultural Intelligence

Cultural intelligence, also known as cultural quotient (CQ), is a foundational link to Diversity, Equity, Inclusion, and Belonging (DEIB). It refers to the ability to be attentive and adaptable in culturally diverse situations, enabling individuals to effectively interact and collaborate with people from different backgrounds. Inclusive leaders display cultural intelligence by valuing and appreciating cultural differences and fostering an environment of inclusivity and belonging.

To be culturally intelligent, inclusive leaders must pay close attention to the experiences and words expressed by others. They actively seek to understand and empathize with individuals from diverse cultures, recognizing the importance of diverse perspectives in driving innovation, creativity, and productivity. By listening and learning from others, inclusive leaders expand their cultural knowledge and develop a deeper understanding of the values, norms, and customs of different cultures.

Moreover, inclusive leaders consciously strive to deepen their cultural understanding and enhance their cultural intelligence. They prioritize cultural learning and expose themselves to various cultural experiences, such as engaging in cross-cultural interactions, attending cultural events, or even learning different languages. Through these efforts, they develop the cognitive component of cultural intelligence, which involves recognizing, understanding, and adapting to different cultures. This cognitive aspect enables inclusive leaders to navigate cultural nuances and make informed decisions that promote cultural diversity and inclusion in their teams and organizations.

They leverage their cultural knowledge and adapt their behavior to respect and appreciate different cultural practices and preferences. This physical intelligence enables inclusive leaders to establish genuine connections and build trust with individuals from diverse cultures, promoting effective collaboration and teamwork.

However, cultural intelligence is not just about knowledge and adaptability; it also requires intrinsic motivation and emotional resilience. Inclusive leaders exhibit emotional and motivational intelligence by developing a strong desire to deepen their cultural understanding, persevering through challenges, and continuously growing their cultural intelligence.

They are driven by a genuine passion for cultural diversity and inclusion, recogn1z1ng the enrichment it brings to their teams and organizations. This emotional and motivational component of cultural intelligence ensures inclusive leaders remain committed to ongoing learning, personal growth, and creating an inclusive and belonging environment for all team members.

To effectively exercise cultural intelligence, inclusive leaders must also be aware of their own experiences and culture, and how these shape their worldview. They acknowledge their biases, assumptions, and stereotypes, and actively challenge them to foster a more inclusive mindset. By reflecting on their own cultural identity and engaging in self-examination, inclusive leaders become more open-minded, empathetic, and culturally sensitive.

Cultural intelligence is a critical component of fostering diversity, equity, inclusion, and belonging within organizations. Inclusive leaders develop their cultural intelligence by actively listening to and learning from individuals from diverse cultures, deepening their cultural understanding, valuing cultural differences, and adapting their behavior to promote inclusion. By incorporating the cognitive, physical, emotional, and self-awareness aspects of cultural intelligence, inclusive leaders create an environment where every individual feels valued, respected, and a sense of belonging, ultimately driving organizational success.

Practical Illustration

Christian is the owner of an insurance company. He is looking for a new manager who is not only proficient with their work, but also displays professional leadership qualities. Most importantly, Christian is looking for a leader who is committed to diversity and inclusion. He decided to ask Sarah, his colleague and close friend, for advice on who to offer the position. Sarah suggested that Elijah would be perfect for the position. She explained that Elijah believes in fairness and equality, and seeks powerful change within the company and outside community. Elijah is not only great for being vocal, but he is excellent at collaborating with others and making sure other voices are heard as well.

Christian listened to Sarah's suggestion. He thought back to a few months ago when Elijah had organized a multicultural potluck for the team, and how great of a bonding experience it was for them. This event allowed everyone to learn more about one another's culture and background, which strengthened the team. Christian thanked Sarah for her advice, and soon made Elijah the new manager. Within weeks, Christian had noticed a positive change in the company. Everyone was happy with Christian's decision, and felt comfortable and respected in the company.

Our ability to reach unity in diversity will be the beauty and test of our civilization. Mahatma Gandhi

Chapter Eight:

Prioritizing DEIB in the Workplace

Every employee is entitled to a work environment that is safe and welcoming. The key to creating a successful and productive workplace is to embrace one another's differences through active steps. When employees are given the opportunities to succeed, they will be happier and more prosperous.

Diversity, Equity, Inclusion, and Belonging will change the entire atmosphere of an organization. In essence, implementing inclusive practices will help to deconstruct barriers of participation and team cohesion. It's important to carefully strategize DEIB practices, in order to create effective long-term changes. Prioritizing DEIB in the workplace is not only beneficial for the well-being of employees, but also for the success of the organization.

Inclusive Recruiting and Hiring

An inclusive work culture requires inclusive hiring. During the recruitment process, it is common for unconscious biases to affect hiring decisions. A recruiter may gravitate towards a particular candidate because of their appearance, background, or connection on a personal level. Inclusive recruiting and hiring involves connecting, recruiting, and offering equal job opportunities to candidates who have the expertise needed for the position from diverse backgrounds. It creates an equitable selection process that eliminates biases.

When the hiring process is inclusive, employees from all different backgrounds will feel supported, and there is a greater effort being put into building a diverse workforce. Inclusive hiring recognizes diversity and embraces the range of perspectives that these individuals can bring into an organization. Ultimately, the team will become stronger and grow efficiently.

Common inclusive hiring practices include:

• Inclusive job advertisements and descriptions: Use inclusive language that is free from gendered terms, jargon, and discriminatory terms. Provide a clear job description that discusses responsibilities.

• An accessible application process and career site: Design an application process that is hassle-free and easy to navigate.

• A diverse interview panel: Choose an appropriate team to help widen your candidate search and get feedback from various perspectives. This will help to eliminate biases.

• Expanding the candidate search: To connect with individuals from different backgrounds, it is beneficial to post job advertisements on various social networks and job boards.

Providing Resources and Accessibility

A work environment should be functional and welcoming for everyone. The consideration of accessibility and proper resources are crucial for creating a culture of inclusivity. When employees arrive to work, they want to feel comfortable and safe. Accommodations can be put in place to meet the needs of employees, and to support any limitations in a proactive way.

Reasonable accommodations can be made to equipment/software, job tasks, schedules, products, or services. Accessibility and resources must be constantly evaluated to ensure that everyone is able to perform the essential functions of their job. Employers should provide their team with communication, structural, and environmental support. When a work space is designed to be accessible to everyone, opportunities are created.

There are many ways an organization can support their employees with accessible designs, accommodations and proper resources, including:

- Having designated handicapped parking spaces

- Doors, hallways, restrooms, and desks that are wide enough to allow for wheelchairs, canes, and walkers
- Accessible buttons and one-touch door opening

- The control of lights, sound, and temperature

- Providing screen-reading software so that a message may be heard, ratherthan read

- Safe accommodations for pregnant employees, such as light duties, modifications, or other reasonable accommodations as requested by the employee

- Designated private areas for nursing mothers, that are not washrooms. This space should include a chair and a flat surface on which to place a breast pump

- Implementing wayfinding, braille lettering, and other graphical cues

- Gender-neutral washrooms

Practice Allyship

An important part of the equity, inclusion, and diversity conversation is allyship. Allyship is a powerful tool for attaining DEIB related change. Being an ally involves learning and listening.

It includes supportive behaviors, actions, and practices, as well as advocating *with* others from underrepresented groups, such as POC (people of color), LGBTQIA+, women, or people with disabilities.

Allyship represents a long-lasting commitment to overcome the systemic barriers that exist. When we support others through allyship, we can work towards creating a safer workplace. Although an ally may not be a part of the marginalized group that they are supporting, they still make the continuous effort of their energy and time. No matter who we are, we all have the potential to become better allies.

To become a better ally in the workplace, consider the following:

- Understand personal privilege, implicit biases, and identity

- Use mistakes as a learning experience and growth

- Educate yourself, rather than waiting to be taught or shown

- Listen with respect and a willingness to learn

- Do the work, every day

- Do not assume that every member of a marginalized community feels oppressed

- Be an upstander, rather than a bystander

Supporting Gender Identity

Embracing the fact that people identify with diverse gender pronouns will help to incorporate equity and inclusion into the organization. Gender identity is an individual's experience of gender, behavior, and expression. The public presentation of how an individual expresses their gender is known as gender expression.

By supporting gender identity in the workplace, it will create a more accepting place for everyone, especially for people who are a part of the LGBTQIA+ community. There are many ways to support diverse gender identities, in which most of it comes down to respect and awareness.

To support gender identity and expression in the workplace, consider:

• Adding pronouns to the email structure: After the name, add "she/her", "he/him", "they/ them". This creates awareness of preferred pronouns and is welcoming to members of the LGBTQIA+ community.

• Provide gender-neutral washrooms: These are washrooms that may be used by any gender.

• Update language on employee forms: When sex or a gendered title is requested, allow for the options of "prefer not to answer" or "other". If possible, have this field be optional. Instead of a gendered title, consider asking for the preferred pronouns.

• Do not make judgments or assumptions of an individual's gender identity: Even if it is done unintentionally, misgendering can be extremely harmful.

• Remove gender from the company dress code: Rather than specifying for employees to wear skirts or suits, state that they must wear professional attire that is most suitable for their position.

Regular Check- Ins - To establish inclusivity, it's important to check-in with employees regularly. Checking-in will help to understand what needs to be changed or improved, as well as the current state of the workplace culture. Inclusivity and equity cannot exist in an environment where they are not encouraged to thrive.

Regular check-ins support a continuous feedback culture that will help to gauge how employees are feeling. It sends the message that everyone is being recognized and heard, through honest conversations. This creates an opportunity to build trust amongst the team. While it is important to check in with team members, it is also important to encourage them to do the same.

Checking-in with employees may be done through:
• One-on-one meetings
• Anonymous employee surveys
• Focus groups that discuss inclusion issues
• Workshops to collect feedback

Practical Illustration

Curtis was looking to hire a new salesperson for his company. He wanted the job advertisement to be inclusive to everyone, so he made sure that it was free from gendered terms and jargon. To connect with a variety of individuals, Curtis posted the job advertisement on different social networks and job boards. Within days, there were many people who had applied for the position. Curtis had chosen a diverse interview panel to help him conduct the interviews, that included his HR representative, and an experienced salesperson who had been in the field for many years.

Rhonda was one of the individuals who had applied to the sales position, and she felt very comfortable entering the interview. She noticed a poster about allyship in the hallway, and was happy that the email from the manager had included preferred pronouns. During the interview, Rhonda had informed Curtis and the team that she is a new mother, and that she had previous sales experience prior to her leave. She went on to have a great interview, and was soon hired for the sales position.

During Rhonda's first week, she was given a designated private area with a place for a breast pump. Curtis had checked in with her to see how she was doing. Rhonda was happy to have entered such a welcoming and inclusive workplace.

We are not a collection of communities from diverse backgrounds to form an alliance; we are one community.

Maya Angelou

Chapter Nine:

Workplace Culture and Policies

Workplace policies are a reflection of what the company values, as well as what they do not value. To improve Diversity, Equity, Inclusion, and Belonging in the workplace, workplace policies can be very influential for creating rules and standards that are fair for every employee. They help to communicate priorities, as well as boundaries. Policies alone will not drive DEIB, but they are an important part of the effort to help foster an inclusive culture. It also takes accountability and transparency to build this culture. When we focus on achieving an inclusive workplace, we can measure our success by tracking workplace diversity.

Writing a DEIB Statement

Defining the company's DEIB initiatives is important. A DEIB statement is an articulation of a company's commitment to furthering diversity, equity, and inclusive practices within their organization. It acknowledges how Diversity, Equity, Inclusion, and Belonging will shape the company's values. However, a DEIB statement is more than a formal, public broadcast to consumers, investors, and employees; it is a driver of change within the company. The efforts to align and communicate a clear DEIB statement involves important conversations within the company, and determines benchmarks to help measure the effects and success.

These important conversations will determine current understandings and ambitions, as well as decisions on actionable steps to move forward. The company is held accountable to their commitments to diversity.

A DEIB statement will present the company's mission and explain how Diversity, Equity, Inclusion, and Belonging connect to their company mission. The statement should reflect on the company's dedication to prioritizing the voices, perspectives, and needs of marginalized groups, as well as their current DEIB efforts and company actions.

When creating a DEIB statement, there are various questions that the company can consider, including:

- Why is this statement important?

- What are our goals that relate to Diversity, Equity, Inclusion, and Belonging?

- How does our organization define these important terms?

- How are DEIB efforts currently incorporated in our company?

- Are all voices heard and considered in the creation of our DEIB Statement?

Zero-Tolerance Policy

As companies continue to strive towards creating inclusive environments, zero- tolerance policies are becoming more common. A zero-tolerance policy prohibits any form of harassment or discrimination, including sexism, homophobia, racism, and ageism. It is intended to help employees feel safe in the workplace, while respecting one another's differences. Additionally, the policy will outline the consequences for not adhering to the policy. Every company is responsible for drafting a zero-tolerance policy that includes important and relevant elements.

Some of these elements include:

- Prohibited behavior: Physical harm to others, discrimination, sexual harassment.

- How to report non-compliance: To whom it should be reported (supervisor, HR), reporting method (hotline or written report).

- Consequences for engaging in such behaviors: Verbal warning, written warning, termination, legal action.

- Company's responsibility: Provide training on the policy, encourage employees to report incidences, enforce punishment for non-adherence.

- Employees' responsibility: Understand the policy, report incidences.

Handling Discrimination Complaints

Discrimination and harassment can severely impact an individual. It can affect the victim mentally, emotionally, and physically. When employees come forward with complaints regarding this behavior, it is crucial to take them very seriously. A discrimination complaint will notify an appropriate authority, whether it is an HR representative, manager or boss, that there has been an act of discrimination. This act of discrimination may have been witnessed, or personally experienced . Employees have the legal right to report these incidences to the appropriate authority in the workplace.

When harassment or discrimination complaints arise, it is important to do the following:

- Address the complaint immediately.
- Listen to the employee with respect and full attention as they provide details on the incident.
- Take every complaint seriously.
- Keep the investigation confidential.
- Conduct a thorough investigation. It may be necessary to hire a third
- party for the investigation.
- Avoid retaliation against the employee or witness.
- Document every step of the investigation.
- Take necessary disciplinary actions against the harasser.

Equal Employment Opportunity

It is every employee's right to receive fair treatment and equal employment, promotions, and training. The Equal Employment Opportunity (EEO) is a principle that is protected by law throughout many countries, and an important concept that every business should practice. It states that every employee, regardless of sex, race, disability, age, or religion, should have the right to work, as well as advance in employment opportunities. The intent is to create a more balanced representation of individuals in the workplace, that prohibits any discrimination, creates awareness about marginalized groups, and promotes equality for everyone.

EEO focuses on improving workplace diversity and creating a positive atmosphere for every team member. This includes recruitment and hiring processes, termination or demotions, compensation, pay scale, and disciplinary measures. The Equal Employment Opportunity does not necessarily mean that an underrepresented group member will automatically get hired, but rather that they will not be rejected simply because they are a part of a particular group.

Recognizing Holidays and Celebrations

An important part of building an inclusive company culture is to recognize the many different holidays and festivities that happen throughout the year. A diverse workplace accepts and accommodates for these differences.

Since every employee has different celebrations and holiday traditions, it is best to take an inclusive approach. This way, everyone will feel respected and welcome. Inclusion involves taking the time to learn about diverse practices, and deciding on best practices to take an inclusive approach to these celebrations. By bringing awareness to diversity and inclusion events, it will help to set a standard for equality in the organization.

To enhance inclusivity with holidays and cultural events, consider the following:

- Have employees share details related to their cultural or religious practices.

- Research diverse holidays.

- Consider rephrasing your holiday greetings.

- Have a diversity calendar as a tool to show religious, cultural, and historical
    events of diverse groups.

- Be fair with time off requests and accommodations.

- Bring awareness to others on diverse holidays.

Practical Illustration

Khadija has been with her company for a couple of months. Her colleagues have been talking about the company's upcoming Christmas party, and they are so excited for Khadija to be able to experience the party. Khadija is happy to be a part of such a friendly and inviting team, however she is nervous to inform them that she cannot attend the Christmas party, as it is on the same day as her Hanukkah celebrations. She is worried that her colleagues might not understand the importance of this celebration. After some thought, Khadija decided to tell her boss, Robert, about her situation.

Robert was happy that Khadija felt comfortable telling him about her concerns. He reminded Khadija that there was a zero-tolerance policy on any forms of discrimination and bullying, and that every employee is entitled to fair treatment. Robert was interested in hearing about Khadija's Hanukkah celebrations, and Khadija was happy to share these details with Robert. After Khadija had left Robert's office, he decided that it would be a good idea to review the company policies and their DEIB statement as a team. Robert wanted every employee to feel welcomed and safe in an inclusive environment, and he knew that required continuous efforts and action.

We are all different, which is great because we are all unique. Without diversity, life would be very boring.

Catherine Pulsifer

Chapter Ten:

Encouraging Respect and Belonging

Encouraging respect and belonging in the workplace is crucial for creating a positive and inclusive environment where each employee feels valued and supported. This essay will explore various strategies and practices that organizations can implement to foster respect and belonging.

Sensitivity training is one effective method that can help employees understand, accept, and respect one another's differences. This type of training focuses on raising awareness of personal biases and prejudices and encourages individuals to transform their thinking to contribute to a more equitable workplace. By addressing issues such as race, gender, religion, and cultural differences, sensitivity training promotes intercultural awareness and enables employees to better understand and interact with people from diverse backgrounds. The goal should be to create a workplace culture where differences are valued and celebrated.

Creating safe spaces within the organization is essential for employees to feel secure and comfortable expressing themselves freely. Safe spaces are free from misconduct, harassment, and abuse, and provide an environment where difficult and important issues can be discussed openly. By offering a place for employees to connect, share ideas, and discuss challenges, safe spaces empower individuals to be authentic without fear of repercussions. It is the responsibility of team leaders and employees at all levels to ensure the creation and maintenance of safe spaces within the workplace.

Emotional intelligence is another critical aspect of encouraging respect and belonging. Emotional intelligence requires individuals to be aware of their own emotions as well as the emotions and needs of others. By developing empathy, individuals can emotionally understand and recognize what others are experiencing or feeling, fostering stronger connections and relationships.

Emotional self-awareness also helps individuals become more aware of their conscious and unconscious biases, enabling them to actively work towards eliminating them. Additionally, emotional intelligence improves mindfulness, allowing individuals to better navigate differences and embrace diversity.

Intentional inclusion is crucial for successful workplace inclusion. It involves deliberate and action-based efforts to promote positive changes in diversity and inclusion practices. Organizations must go beyond teaching employees about inclusion and implement procedures to ensure its practice. Without intentional inclusion, the risk of unintentional exclusion arises. Creating a flexible and open culture that overcomes challenges such as conflict, communication, and change requires collective effort.

Every individual must work together to create positive changes in diversity, equity, inclusion, and belonging within the workplace. Expressing appreciation is another powerful way to foster respect and belonging in the workplace. Recognition and rewards not only drive employee engagement but also contribute to building an inclusive culture. It is important for organizations to ensure that every employee is recognized for their contributions and actions. Meaningful recognition that highlights specific accomplishments and values individuals for who they are creates a sense of value and respect. By implementing a well-designed recognition system, organizations can celebrate diversity and create a culture that encourages authenticity and inclusion.

Encouraging respect and belonging in the workplace is essential for creating a positive and inclusive environment. Sensitivity training, safe spaces, emotional intelligence, intentional inclusion, and expressing appreciation are all effective strategies that organizations implement to foster respect and belonging. By valuing and celebrating diversity, organizations can create a culture where every employee's voice is heard and where individuals feel a sense of belonging, leading to increased productivity, engagement, and success.

How does intentional inclusion play a role in promoting diversity and inclusion within an organization, and what actions can be taken to make inclusion a deliberate effort?

Intentional inclusion refers to the deliberate and proactive effort to foster diversity and inclusion within an organization. It helps ensure that individuals from different backgrounds, perspectives, and experiences feel welcome, valued, and engaged. By making inclusion a deliberate effort, organizations can tap into the benefits of diversity, enhance employee morale and retention, and drive innovation and creativity.

To promote intentional inclusion within an organization, several actions can be taken:

1. Leadership commitment: Leadership should emphasize the importance of inclusion and communicate it as a core value. This commitment must be actively demonstrated through words and actions.

2. Diverse hiring practices: Organizations should implement inclusive hiring policies that attract a wide range of candidates. This can be done by widening the recruitment pool, creating job descriptions that eliminate bias, utilizing diverse interview panels, and providing equal opportunities for underrepresented groups.

3. Inclusive workplace culture: Foster an environment that values diversity and encourages the contribution of all employees. Emphasize open communication, respectful dialogue, and understanding of different perspectives. Establish policies and procedures that address any discriminatory behaviors and promote inclusivity.

Metrics and accountability: Establish measurable goals and regularly track progress towards diversity and inclusion benchmarks. Hold leaders and managers accountable for achieving these objectives and foster a culture of transparency and continuous improvement.

Partnerships and outreach: Engage in community partnerships and outreach initiatives that promote diversity and inclusion. This can include collaborating with diverse suppliers, participating in diversity-focused events, and supporting charitable organizations that align with the organization's values.

By taking these deliberate steps, organizations can actively promote a more inclusive environment that celebrates diversity and harnesses the benefits of varied perspectives, ultimately leading to a more innovative and successful organization. Organizations can adopt several strategies to prioritize intentional inclusion in their diversity and inclusion initiatives, leading to a positive impact on the overall organizational culture. Here are a few strategies:

What strategies can organizations adopt to prioritize intentional inclusion in their diversity and inclusion initiatives, and how can these efforts positively impact the overall organizational culture?

1. **Leadership Commitment:** Ensure that senior leadership demonstrates their commitment to intentional inclusion by setting clear goals, expectations, and holding themselves accountable. This commitment sends a message throughout the organization about the importance and value of diversity and inclusion.

2. **Regular Feedback and Evaluation:** Establish mechanisms for employees to provide feedback on the organization's diversity and inclusion initiatives. Regularly assess progress, identify gaps, and make adjustments accordingly. Encourage open dialogue and communication channels to address concerns and suggestions for improvement.

These intentional inclusion strategies can positively impact the overall organizational culture in several ways:

1. **Increased Innovation and Creativity:** By fostering a diverse and inclusive environment, organizations benefit from diverse perspectives, experiences, and ideas. This diversity of thought stimulates innovation and creativity, enabling organizations to find unique solutions to complex problems.

2. **Enhanced Employee Engagement and Retention:** Inclusive organizations create a sense of belonging and psychological safety, where employees feel valued and respected. This leads to higher employee engagement levels and improved retention rates.

3. **Improved Decision-Making:** Diverse teams make better decisions by considering multiple viewpoints and avoiding groupthink. Intentional inclusion ensures diverse voices are heard and valued in decision-making processes, leading to more effective and well- rounded outcomes.

4. **Expanded Market Reach:** Inclusive organizations reflect the diversity of their customer base, enabling them to better understand and serve a wide range of customers. This can lead to increased customer satisfaction, loyalty, and business growth.

5. **Enhanced Reputation and Employer Branding:** Organizations that prioritize intentional inclusion and demonstrate their commitment to diversity and inclusion initiatives build a positive reputation externally. This improves their employer branding, attracting top talent who seek inclusive work environments.

Overall, by embracing intentional inclusion, organizations can create a more vibrant, inclusive, and high-performing culture that celebrates diversity, fosters innovation, and drives business success.

What specific steps can organizations take to foster intentional inclusion in their recruitment, hiring, and promotion processes?

There are several specific steps organizations can take to foster intentional inclusion in their recruitment, hiring, and promotion processes. Here are some key actions they can implement:

1. **Develop inclusive job descriptions:** Craft job descriptions that focus on qualifications and skills rather than educational background or specific experience that could unintentionally exclude certain groups. Use gender-neutral language and emphasize a commitment to diversity and inclusion.

2. **Implement blind recruitment techniques:** Remove any identifiable information (such as name, gender, age, and ethnicity) from resumes during the initial screening process. This reduces unconscious bias and ensures candidates are shortlisted based solely on their qualifications.

3. **Train hiring managers and recruiters:** Provide training to those involved in the recruitment process on unconscious bias, diversity and inclusion, and fair hiring practices. This helps to raise awareness and develop skills for unbiased candidate assessment.

4. **Establish diverse interview panels:** Ensure that interview panels are made up of individuals from diverse backgrounds. This can help provide different perspectives and minimize bias during the evaluation process.

5. **Actively source candidates from diverse talent pools:** To attract a wider range of candidates, actively seek individuals from underrepresented groups and minority communities. Partner with diverse organizations, attend career fairs focused on diverse talent, or use online platforms that specialize in diversity recruitment.

6. **Create affinity groups or additional employee resource groups (ERGs):** Establish affinity groups that bring together employees with shared backgrounds, interests, or experiences. These groups provide support, networking opportunities, and can serve as a resource for attracting and retaining diverse talent.

7. **Implement diversity goals and metrics:** Set specific goals for diversity and inclusion within the organization and regularly measure progress using metrics. This ensures accountability and helps identify areas for improvement.

8. Review promotion processes for bias: Analyze promotion criteria and processes to identify any potential biases. For example, consider whether there are specific requirements or expectations that disproportionately disadvantage certain groups.

9. Provide unconscious bias training for decision-makers: Train managers and decision-makers on identifying and addressing unconscious bias during promotion processes. This helps to ensure that individuals are assessed based on their merits and potential rather than any biases.

10. Foster an inclusive company culture: Creating an overall environment that values diversity and inclusion is essential for attracting and retaining diverse talent. Encourage employee resource groups, organize diversity and inclusion training sessions, and make diversity a part of the organization's mission and values.

By implementing these steps, organizations can work towards intentional inclusion throughout their talent acquisition and promotion processes, leading to a more diverse and equitable workplace.

Closing Thoughts

"Too many of us still believe our differences define us."
- **John Lewis**

"It's just really important that we start celebrating our differences. Let's start tolerating first, but then we need to celebrate our differences." -   **Billie Jean King**

"Strength lies in differences, not in similarities." - **Stephen covey**

www.ingramcontent.com/pod-product-compliance
Lightning Source LLC
Chambersburg PA
CBHW070923290526
45795CB00001B/403